Aria of a Brown Girl

Also By Sarita Vargas:
My Adoption Story, Parts 1 & 2
www.saritasiren.com

Aria of a Brown Girl

By Sarita Vargas

Aria of a Brown Girl

Copyright © 2023 by Sarita Vargas

All rights reserved. No part of this book may be reproduced or transmitted in any form or by any means without written permission from the author.

ISBN: 979-8-218-15939-9

Published in the USA by Siren Songs, LLC

Author photo by Kristen Aronen

Dust jacket designed by Devante Vargas

DEDICATION

For my first loves, my children:

Strong, handsome, and kind Anthony, it's an honor and a pleasure to be your mom. You never cease to impress me with your steady climb to the top of the mountains that hold your dreams. Keep going kiddo, you can do it.

Beautiful, strong, and unique Chloe, my sunshine girl, my adventurous child-turned-best friend. I love our daily chats and your wise insight to life's mysteries. You are significant. Remember to take time for you.

Quick and so-cool Joey, thank you for including me in your life, and for sharing your moments with me. Your kind ways and your laugh make me smile, and I love you exactly the way you are. Be true to yourself, and don't ever hide you.

Brave and honest Brianna, you are the one who I never have to guess with. You're scary in all the best ways. You're a straight shooter, and nothing gets by your sharp eye. I love that about you. Trust your instincts and keep your heart tender.

Artsy and mysterious Jadzia, my bonus child, my dark faerie, who accepted me without question. I am so pleased to know you, and so thankful for the opportunity to love you. You matter in this world, don't lose sight of your muchness.

For my mom and dad, who adopted me and loved me as their own. You gave me the foundation I would need in life to successfully rise above my trauma one day. You loved me through every phase of life, and never gave up on the hope that one day I would find peace and healing. You took many afflictions that were not your own, and bore them for me… I see that now. Thank you.

For my mom, my dear birth mom. You were there for me when I needed you the most. You gave me life, and I'll love you forever. You have loved me for me, and the world is such a better place with you in it. You're delicate like rain, and inspiring like the sun. This quote reminds me of you: "My mother told me to be a lady. And for her, that meant be your own person, be independent." ~ Ruth Bader Ginsburg

....

For Kimmy, who throughout all these years, will forever be my Duckie. The one person who accepted no excuses, but at the same time gave understanding— that's my Kimmy. Without your kindness and direction, I would have been completely lost.

For my Kristen, my "sister wife," who ended up being my person. Never had I had anyone tell me to just be me, and the rest of the world can just deal with it. You have known just about all my flaws, and not once did you judge me. You opened your heart, your family, and your home to me without question, and for that I will always be grateful.

For Kevin, you saved me in the moments when I could not save myself. You stuck by my side and decided to be my dear friend through all of life's storms— because when the sun came out, it was magic. Our friendship means the world to me.

*Last but **definitely not** least, my husband:*

Devante, the man whose support is continuous, and whose love is unconditional, and without whom, I would not have the guts and guile to share my story. Devante, I love you so much, and because of you, I finally understand what it means to love and be loved the way I deserve. It's you. It's always been you. It will forever be you, times infinity, no backs.

PREFACE

"Now is the time for guts and guile." ~ Elizabeth Taylor

This book is written in three parts. The first part is written in a different style than the second and third. You see, the first part is written as I remember life back then: moments of time, pieces of memories that have stuck in my brain. I don't remember much about my very young years, mainly the parts where I was introduced to a world that never should have existed for me, or anyone. There are humorous moments sprinkled in, for comic relief, or maybe for my own self and the need to take a break from the other things, I don't know. As the book progresses, it becomes a story as my memory is a bit clearer and instead of things happening to me, it became the shape my life took because of the things I experienced.

There have been numerous times I have put my laptop away, tears streaming from my eyes, wondering if I could even finish this labor of love. There have been times where I remember things that up until now, I forgot about, and the memories hit me like a brick. There were times I debated even sharing any of this, for fear that I would bring shame upon my family, or perhaps I would lose friends who weren't able to accept my past. It was during those times, I reminded myself that my story is important, and for the survivors of abuse, it needs to be told. Any friends I lose along the way, are not friends to begin with, and I am better off having no ties to them any longer.

I ask you to read this book with an open heart, an open mind, a kind understanding, and an appreciation for the guts and guile it took to write this. Although at times, my language is "colorful", and the situations I found myself in are sometimes described in a graphic manner, I am trying to keep true to who I was, who I became, who I wanted to be, and who I am now. I make no apologies for my story, but I do want you, the reader, to know that I mean no offense. I implore you to look past your own aversion to unpleasant things, so that you will be able to really know me.

Stay with me, there is a burst of song in healing. You will see.

*Most names and places may have been changed to protect the innocent, the wicked, and/or the people who might sue me. I would also like to acknowledge that while these memories are solely my own, and while my memories may be imperfect, I have done my best to assure they are the truth as I remember it. I acknowledge that the people, friends, and family members in my story may have conflicting memories of events, places, and times. I do not wish to imply that the memories of my family, friends or otherwise are untrue; at the same time, I wish to convey that mine are as truthful as I am able to recall.

Aria: a soaring piece of music for solo voice, most often with the backup of a full orchestra. Arias usually make their appearance between dramatic scenes and are a reflection of the character's emotions.

Table of Contents

VIOLATIONS -- 1

The Girl & the Kiss --- 3

The Girl on the Farm --- 11

The Girl & the Frying Pan -- 23

The Girl & the Frog -- 31

The Girl & the Highball -- 35

The Girl & the Reunions -- 39

The Girl & the Lost Week --- 43

The Girl & the Condom --- 49

The Girl & the Minivan --- 55

The Girl & the California Boy -- 61

The Girl & the Football Player -- 67

The Girl Goes Bananas -- 73

The Girl Arrives -- 81

The Girl & the Aria -- 91

The Girl, Funny Guy, & the Surfer ------------------------------------- 97

The Girl, NWA, Mary Jane & the Cop -------------------------------- 107

The Girl, the Rave, & Vibrating Guy ---------- 117

The Girl Goes to Vegas ---------- 125

THE AFTERMATH ---------- **128**

The Girl Gets to Eat ---------- 131

The Girl is a Mom ---------- 141

The Girl, the New Job, & An "Oops" ---------- 157

The Girls Slings Drinks ---------- 167

The Girl Has UPS, & Downs ---------- 175

The Girl & the Crack in the Universe ---------- 183

The Girl & Questionable Happenings ---------- 189

The Girl & A Daughter's Wish ---------- 195

The Girl, An Old Flame, & the Sister Wife ---------- 203

The Girl, the Ghosts, & The Golden Boy ---------- 215

The Girl & the Playing Field ---------- 227

The Girl & Karma's Visit ---------- 237

The Girl Gets Schooled on Grief ---------- 241

HEALING ---------- **244**

A Different Kind of Love, Mate ---------- 245

Her Culture, Their New York ---------- 257

One Dream at a Time ---------- 265

We Are All in This Together ---------- 275

Aria ---------- 281

Violations

The Girl & the Kiss

I was five years old when I received my first grown-up kiss. Later, in middle school, I would lie and say it was from Danny Sims in the seventh grade. I knew even then that what happened to me as a trusting little girl was unseemly, but I couldn't tell anyone; that was out of the question. I had no idea that would only be the beginning of numerous unwelcome sexual advances throughout my young life.

I grew up in a strict Christian home, and you could find us at church Sunday mornings, Sunday evenings, and Wednesday evenings come hell or high water. There we were, sitting in the pew, singing the old hymns, and then listening to the pastor. I was at church for what feels like the first 11 years of my life. Our church was in an old school building on top of a hill in McKinley, Minnesota. The space was also used for our church's Christian School, called McKinley Christian Academy. I attended, along with just about every other kid in the congregation.

McKinley Christian Academy was originally for grades K-12. I'm not sorry I attended church school; I feel like I learned a lot of things there that helped me later in life. However, it wasn't without rules that

I found to be hypocritical at worst and tedious at best.

We had to wear dresses every day to school, come fall, winter, or spring. For gym class, we would put pants under our skirts. Skirts and dresses had to be below the knee, nothing to suggest worldliness was allowed. Boys usually wore slacks and not jeans. It wasn't a rule, per se, but it was a strong expectation. I so wanted to wear jeans; I loved jeans. I hated dresses, I was always cold in them. Some days, I would have to wear tights under the dress or skirt, and I developed rashes behind my knees from how much they itched. I also had a smashing pair of saddle shoes, along with some brown ones with crocodiles or alligators on them. I wanted some cool shoes, but that wasn't in the budget nor was it considered important. So off to school I went, usually in my parent's station wagon or the minibus, all dressed up in my homemade dresses and saddle shoes. You read that right— I wore homemade dresses. My mom lovingly sewed my clothes, whether out of necessity or enjoyment, I am not entirely sure. Maybe it was both, and at the time, I didn't know anything other than that. There were patterns by Simplicity, McCall's, Butterick, take your pick.

We also received "demerits." Demerits were a tally system at the school that ended up in spankings. If you misbehaved, you received a demerit. If you talked out of turn too many times, yup, another demerit. If you didn't do your homework, or you didn't have your parent sign your bad grade on an assignment, you guessed it— you got a demerit. Once you received a few demerits, you were the winner of a spanking with the paddle. The paddle was wooden and shaped like a very short canoe paddle, but with holes in the wide flat part for easy motion. You would get three, and it was not a fun experience. I received a spanking once or twice in school. It was horrible because not only was it humiliating, but it was awkward having to be in front of an adult you didn't know, with your ass in the air as you bent forward.

We all brown-bagged it for lunch, there were no hot lunches at my school. My mom was one of those moms. She always had to feed us something healthy, when all I wanted was a PB&J with Doritos, or maybe cookies. I would die for fruit roll-ups or some of the other crap my friend's moms packed them; Jell-O pudding cups, anything. But no, instead, good ol' mom insisted on packing us a wholesome meal of some sort of sandwich on brown bread, a handful of carrots, a banana, (usually bruised and super ripe) and, if we were "really lucky," Fig-fucking-Newtons. Pardon my swearing. I think I swear a lot because swearing wasn't allowed in our house. Every now and then I heard my dad say, "Doggone it!" That was only if he was super mad, otherwise he would just fume, clench his teeth, and say nothing. Let's get back to the lunches. Sometimes I talked my friend Rachel into sharing her snickerdoodles with me. Rachel was my best friend besides Jake, and she would always have some scrumptious, fresh-baked bakery in her lunch. I think her mom baked all the time, because Rachel was pretty "sturdy" until her adult years. I loved that about her.

Another thing that plagued me about being in a small private school, was the fact that I was adopted. I had known this about myself for as long as I could remember. My mother would tell me the story of me; she would do it in such a loving way, that although I felt like I was different, I did feel loved by my parents very much. Being adopted, I obviously didn't look like them, especially my dad. He was Norwegian and thus, blond, and blue-eyed. He had light skin, and so did his side of the family. My adoptive mom was, in fact, Mexican- like me, so I looked a little bit like her. Even though my mom was a lighter-skinned Mexican, she was darker than most of the women in the area we lived in. She didn't have an accent, as her parents taught her English as a first language. She could speak Spanish, but we never heard it at home.

I was brown, with long, jet-black hair that was so black, it gave off a blue sheen. I also had big teeth and stick-out ears. You learn early on that if you're brown-skinned in a sea of white, you get asked "why is your skin like that" or "what are you" or "are you Indian?" This boy I had the misfortune of having a crush on would ask me, "What tribe are you from," especially if my hair was braided. I begged and begged my parents to let me have short hair, this way it couldn't be braided, pony-tailed, or pulled back in any way. For three years, all my pleading was for naught; I wouldn't get my short hair until a bit later in elementary school. Oh, how I hated my brown skin, my blue-black hair, and my stick-out ears. I just wanted to be cute and blonde or at least have light-brown hair like the rest of the girls in class.

Being adopted and not knowing anything about my birth mom meant I could imagine I was anything. Once I went to school and told everyone I was French. Being French sounded so cool and sophisticated. I don't know if anyone believed me. I got a few stares, but no one volunteered any praises or asked me anything about France, so I made it through the rest of the day mostly unscathed. That wouldn't always be the case.

I was in Kindergarten I think, maybe 1st grade, and I was at my personal desk space when the urge to pee hit me. Now, we had little flags that we would insert in a small hole at the top ledge of our desk; blue flag for a question, yellow flag if we needed to use the rest room. I don't know why I waited until last minute, but finally, I put my yellow flag up. My teacher was busy helping another kid named Justin. I never liked Justin and the fact that he was the reason my bladder was bursting without release was not lost on me; I just hated him even more. I grabbed my yellow flag and waved it above my head rather vigorously, but the teacher seemed to take her time getting over to my desk to give me permission to get up and go.

I stopped looking at my flag pleadingly, because the yellow color was making me need go even more. Finally, I could no longer contain the waterfall of urine that I had been holding for what seemed like forever. There it went, all down my tights, the side of my chair, and onto a puddle on the hardwood floor beneath me. I blamed Justin. I blamed my teacher. I blamed the school. I blamed the stupid flag rule. My teacher ended up rushing me out of the classroom, and somehow, I had dry clothes to change into and the floor got cleaned. Later I told everyone it wasn't me that peed. I blamed it on Chad, the poor the kid that sat next to me. He was the peeing criminal, not me, I told them. A few of my friends seemed to believe me, I don't know if they really did or if they were just coming to my rescue. In any case, I think this is when my battle with dehydration started. To this day I don't like drinking water and I'm terrified of peeing my pants.

My mom was a teacher at the Christian school. She taught

penmanship class. Yes, that was a class back then, and even now my mom loves to write lists. There we would sit, swooping our endings on certain words and looping our loops just so. The letters needed to be slanted properly, and of course be the proper height. People don't really write in cursive anymore; I find that I still rather enjoy it.

Because my mom was a teacher, we would often stay after school on Wednesdays, because that was church night. Before the evening service, we would get to eat dinner with Mrs. Erb, the sweet older lady that lived in our church building. She had an apartment there, and she also taught school. She was widowed, and the church took care of her. Mrs. Erb was a fantastic cook. Absolutely nothing went to waste, so she would come up with all kinds of uses for what she had in her fridge. There was dandelion salad, scrapple, and Mexican lasagna, all things I grew to love, as we ate at her home countless times over the years.

I'm pretty sure school ended around 3 p.m., so I would have between 3:00 and about 4:30 to kind of wander the school or play outside if it was nice weather. Our sermons would be in the gymnasium, and people would arrive early to set up all the chairs for service. After church, the chairs got stacked up again so the gym could be used for school during the week.

On one such Wednesday afternoon, I believe I was in kindergarten, or first grade, I found myself wandering around the school, gleefully going up and down the floors, when I ended up in the gymnasium. I grabbed a basketball and shot hoops by myself, pretending to be a superstar athlete, when I saw the side door swing open and one of the older boys from school sauntered in. He was a teenager, and I dribbled as I watched him take a seat on one of the chairs that would later be set out for church service. I felt self-conscious as he just sat there watching me. Eventually, he beckoned me over, and being as he was older, I obediently went. I don't remember every single second of that moment, but I do remember him coaxing me to sit on his lap. I thought it was strange that he would want that, and after a short time, I reluctantly obeyed.

So, there was little me in my homemade gingham dress, on the lap of this teenage boy, with my legs dangling over the right side of him. The next thing I remember is him telling me to kiss him. Just one kiss, he promised. At this point I wasn't exactly afraid … I was confused more than anything. Why did this big teenager want me to kiss him? At length, because he seemed to be begging, I finally decided I better kiss him, just to get him to stop. I leaned in to kiss his cheek and was surprised when he turned his head and was suddenly facing me. This was the first time I felt alarm flood my body, and it made me want to jump down from my perch. As it was, he had a gentle but solid grip around my waist, so for the time being, I was immobile.

It didn't end up being a peck on the cheek the way my dad did it, or a quick peck on the other cheek the way my mom did it. His kiss was directly on my lips, and I felt his tongue touching the inside of my mouth. I am pretty sure I froze. Finally, after what seemed like forever, I was able to wriggle free of his firm grip. I felt scared, wrong, panicked even, and I hopped down, terrified. I ignored his husky sounding pleading with me to stay, and instead ran out of the gym, seeking the comfort and safety of Mrs. Erb's apartment.

All that evening I fearfully thought about that kiss. I knew there was something about it that was hazy, and fuzzy, wrong, and weird. I felt like I had sinned, and I didn't dare tell anyone for fear that I would get a spanking. There was no kissing outside of marriage you know, not in this church, not in my family, or anyone's family. Was I married now and just didn't know it? I was horror-stricken, and so I packed up that moment, and filed it away with all the other moments that were weird, fuzzy, hazy, and panicky.

The Girl on the Farm

I was always a "town girl" growing up. I didn't like being in the country, and when my parents moved us to the lake house when I was in 9th grade, I thought I would die. It was kind of comical. All the kids in my class would "go to the cabin" on the weekends and they would come back talking about waterskiing, tubing, and "being at the lake" like it was the best thing in the world. I lived on a lake and all I could wish for was one weekend in the city. Not Virginia, the town that was biggest in the area, but something like Duluth, or Minneapolis even. I just wanted to get away from the country. I'm not particularly outdoorsy, in fact, I'm not outdoorsy at all, not even a smidge.

This may sound like I was an unthankful girl. Maybe I was. Or maybe I was just a girl who didn't like the woods, didn't like the dark lake water, didn't like frogs or reptiles, didn't like worms, mice, bugs, or the incredible darkness that falls on a country night. Yet there I was, stuck in an area that had all the above. My opinion didn't matter at all of course. It was always my mom's dream to live on a lake. I think to her it represented calmness, leisure, fun, and status. My dad loved the lake as well, and it was probably a joint dream. I also think he wanted to make my mom happy; "happy wife, happy life" and all that. My brother also liked the lake, as he loved to waterski and speed across the waves in our boat, so it was three against one anyway.

I realize how incredibly spoiled I sound. I don't mean to sound unthankful for a set up that many kids would dream of. Being in these surroundings left me feeling very exposed. I tried waterskiing, and was even good at it, but in truth, I hated it. If you fell, you were out in the middle of the lake where there were often tall weeds that would wrap around your legs. I didn't like lake swimming that much because you couldn't see, and it was dark waters. The wooden ladder going up to the dock was always slippery, who knows what from. Ducks would often swim by, and that left me feeling like the water was dirty. Don't get me started on frogs and the occasional leech. All of this was too much for a girl who had already experienced too much, and only added to the anxiety I was feeling and hiding. Instead, I came across as a brat, hiding out in my room on the second floor with the window overlooking the beautiful lake below.

Despite my dislike for everything "outdoors," I was confused by the beauty of my surroundings. The lake was haunting and cozy feeling in winter. In February, the ice would crack, and you would hear the most deep, frightening, lonely and bizarre echo that would travel from one end of the lake to the other. When spring came, the sun would shine bright on the blinding snow that covered the lake, and little by little, you would see the ice lose out to the warmth of the April temperatures. When summer finally arrived, the trees surrounding the lake were emerald-green, and the loons would call to each other on still and balmy evenings. In the fall, there would be the smell of autumn leaves all around us, and the lake would be so still that it looked like glass, with a few colored leaves laying delicately on its surface.

Yet there I was, terrified of it all, and wishing I were anywhere else. The lake gets blamed for a lot of my discomfort; it was this huge bubble I felt trapped in. I now recognize that the lake was only the scapegoat for everything else I was experiencing at that time in my life on the Iron Range of Minnesota. The Iron Range is the name for a string of little close-knit towns, consisting of Hibbing, Chisholm, Mountain Iron, Virginia, Eveleth, Gilbert, Biwabik, Aurora and Hoyt Lakes. Everything has to do with mining iron ore, and all the towns look like small-town America. It was in this place that I experienced most of the trauma that would wreak havoc on my life.

Like I complained about earlier, I had the kind of mother that made us nutritious meals. She always made sure we ate something healthy, none of that sugar cereal or fruit in a cup nonsense. If we had cereal, it was Raisin Bran or those wheat things that literally felt like straw when you broke them apart and soaked them in milk. We had Grape Nuts cereal and sometimes if mom was in a generous mood - Corn Pops. All I wanted was Boo Berry Cereal, the kind that came out at Halloween, with the ghost on the cover and little blue ghost marshmallows in it. I received some from my dad for Christmas one year and I was so grateful. Why couldn't we have Lucky Charms on the regular like my friends did? Why did we have to have oatmeal or an egg? And always fruit on the side. My mom was big on fruit. Looking back on all of this, I can say with absolute certainty that she cared about our health and was a 5-star mom. At the time though, it felt like torture.

In keeping with healthy, natural foods, another phase my parents went through, was buying unpasteurized cow's milk from a local farm. It tasted revoltingly sweet, and even grassy, and the scent made my stomach lurch. To my relief, my parents took pity on me and would buy me store-bought milk. I was so thankful, because for them to do that was not in keeping with their usual "eat what is put in front of you" thought process. When I think of fresh farm milk, it makes me envision cows and dirty cow udders and the smells and the sounds of the cattle lowing in the meadow. However, those things aren't the worst thoughts it brings to my mind. Dairy farms remind me of an incident that happened a long time ago…

Before we moved to the lake, we lived in Aurora. My parents knew a few people who lived on farms outside of the town, and one night we found ourselves visiting a rather large family at their farmhouse. This was a family that was a bit of a name around the area. They had cows on their farm, and you could hear them as you drove down the driveway.

At this point in my life, I was a very little girl, maybe five years of age, and I knew the rules, especially the main one: "Children should be seen and not heard." You just don't bother the grown-ups over anything really, and you stay out of sight and let the big people visit. So, there we were at this farm, and I was downstairs with all the other kids. I was the youngest, most of the "kids" were teenagers and maybe even young adults. They were all watching something on the TV, I don't remember what it was. I just remember the couch was not big enough and I was squished next to an older teenage boy. I kept looking around at all the big kids, kind of feeling happy that I was down there with all of them. I tried to be quiet so they wouldn't notice me and make me feel like a baby.

It was quite dark, and as I sat there, I became aware of the boy to my left that I was wedged up against. I recognized him as one of the farm owner's sons. I could hear him breathing kind of weird, but it wasn't so loud that anyone else noticed. Out of nowhere, he slowly reached over and grabbed my hand. I sat there, wondering why in the world he would want to hold my hand. I barely knew him, and he was a teenager! I could feel my heart starting to pound loudly in my chest as I contemplated what to do. Do I pull away? Would I get in trouble for being rude? Was this going to be like the kiss I had experienced in the school gym?

As I sat there scrambling for an answer, the question was answered for me. He proceeded to take my hand and slip it across his lower stomach, which was hard and slightly hairy. I became paralyzed. My instincts were right- this was **not** good! I quit breathing, and as I sat there motionless from terror, he pushed my hand further down, **under** his jeans, where I could feel his erect penis. I don't know **how** I knew that's what it was, but I knew that's what it was. He proceeded to try and get me to **really** feel it, and for a second or two, while I sat there frozen to the spot, he moved my hand back and forth on it. Then, as if snapped back to motion, I yanked my hand away, and full of shame and panic, I sprang up off the couch.

Trying to calm myself, I slowly made my way toward the stairs, hoping no one would notice me as I crept out of the family area. The kids were all deeply absorbed in what they were watching, and I could feel a lump forming at the base of my throat. *Don't cry, don't cry, don't cry,* I chanted to myself as I climbed the stairs. If I cried, someone would ask me what was wrong, and I would probably be in trouble. When I got my urge to cry under control, the chant in my mind changed to *don't puke, don't puke, don't puke.*

Once in the light and safety of the upstairs, I found my mom among the rest of the adults in the living room. I went to her side and sat down quietly, begging God to put it in her head to just let me sit with her and not "shoo" me back to the basement. I promised God I would be good, and I would behave, if only my mom would let me stay. Under most circumstances, she **would** have "shooed" me away to the basement, but on this occasion, she let me sit by her, even though there were only adults around. I sat there as quiet as a mouse, not making a peep, hoping to blend into the carpet.

We ended up leaving not too long after that, and as our car left the drive, I could hear the cattle again, and smell the sweetness of the hay and the putrid stench of manure all blending into one stomach turning scent. **That** is what raw cow's milk tasted like to me, **that** is why I couldn't stand drinking it or smelling it. That scent took over a part of my brain associated with being forced to fondle an older boy's penis, and I loathed the memory.

I didn't tell my parents of this memory until much later, when I was in my 30's I believe. Growing up in the environment I grew up in did not lend itself to confiding these things. There was no touching, no sex, no heavy kissing outside of Holy Matrimony complete with God's blessing. I didn't want to be in trouble for my sins. Getting in trouble was the worst, and I just knew I would be in trouble for these things that happened to me. In my immature brain, I didn't realize that I would have never actually been in trouble for being molested. At the time, I didn't know that what was happening to me was sexual abuse, and if I had confided in my parents, they would have helped me. I'm not sure what they would have done, they didn't get the chance to do anything.

When you raise a child in a purist environment, you condition them to think that anything associated with sex is a sin. You condition them to fear the consequences rather than tell someone what is happening to you. There is no gray area, only black and white. I was watching a TikTok... ok, ok, ok. Before you judge me, let me tell you that for every ridiculous thing you see on that app, there are plenty of truths I've seen as well. People have a platform to explain beliefs from another point of view.

Now, in this TikTok, the TikTokker was referencing the Josh Duggar conviction of child pornography and his molestation of young girls, namely, his younger sisters. The Duggar clan participates in **extreme** conservative "Independent Christian" beliefs, which, arguably are considerably stricter than the upbringing I had. I agree with this TikTokker, in relation to the Josh Duggar situation and many other instances of sexual abuse that are similar and go unreported.

Here goes, and I warn you, this is a viewpoint that many of you older-generation, religious adults may find offensive. Arguably, without giving true consideration, different viewpoints are often offensive or scary to many. Here is the TikTok verbatim:

"I'm going to say something that is uncomfortable. So, before you react, please take a minute to regulate your nervous system:

Purity culture encourages pedophilia. Some of the standards of purity culture are:

- Innocence, which pretty much means ignorance about sex.
- Submission, which for women is specifically submission to men.
- Virginity as the ultimate standard of worth, and
- Modesty, which for women means that we are not allowed to wear anything that reveals our adult curves.

Purity culture makes the desirable standard a child, it makes childlikeness desirable in regards (sic) to sexuality. It makes virginity and innocence and submission what the male brain should want most in a partner, and your brain doesn't rewire just because you get married.

This doesn't mean that every man raised in purity

culture is a pedophile. That's not at all what I'm saying. What I'm saying is that purity culture wires the brain of men to desire childlikeness, which encourages pedophilia. After all, desire and objectification happen in our brain.

Now, if you are a pedophile who wants to act on those desires, purity culture does a lot of the grooming for you. Purity culture discourages comprehensive sex education, leaving children without the ability to know what's appropriate and what's not. It shames people for any sexual thoughts or behaviors, which makes children who may be vulnerable not want to tell their caregivers or anybody else if something happens to them. Its emphasis on virginity makes abused children prefer to lie so as not to be seen as less-than. It teaches children not to 'trust their own heart,' and to trust authority figures, which makes any pedophile's voice more important than their own intuition.

It puts responsibility on women to protect men, causing abused girls to blame themselves for the abuse that they are subjected to. If as a society, we really are concerned about vulnerable children, then we need to toss purity culture, advocate for comprehensive sex education, and stop pushing narratives of what desirable women and men should look or behave like; normalize sexuality as a part of the human experience, teach consent to children, talk about sex as a coping mechanism versus a healthy experience, give children agency over their own bodies, which means allowing them to say no to things that you may want them to be ok with, and dismantle absurd notions that virginity and worth are connected.

Women inside fundamentalist Christianity are also expected to depend financially on men, to be home while men are out in the world, to not get formal education. They are expected to be grown children, dependents. Assertive, educated women are 'problematic' and 'not attractive.'

If we really want to protect children and women, then purity culture has to go."

~@joluehmann 12/09/21

Now, I'm going to say a few things regarding the video. The first is, I do not agree with every one of her videos- as a whole. There are plenty of things she says that I do not agree with. Even this video doesn't have my full 100% concurrence. However, this is one video that for me, contains a few harsh truths.

My experience with sex education was non-existent. We were to simply "abstain." If we obeyed and abstained, there was no reason to teach sex education. We weren't supposed to be having sex, so there was no need to be educated about it. I didn't necessarily need to be told "how it was done," I needed to be told that it was ok to tell an adult "*NO*" in a scenario where they were about to ask or demand something from me sexually. I needed to be told that I would not get in trouble if I said, "No" to authority in this case, and that it would not be my fault if it happened despite my saying no, I needed to be told it was ok to say, "No" to a peer, someone my age in a scenario where I felt uncomfortable. I didn't need to be "nice" and be "liked."

I grew up knowing that for girls, physical contact with a boy or a man was just out of the question. I grew up being taught that you respect authority with absolute humbleness and meekness. Even my dad would sometimes put my mother in her place. It wasn't often, and it wasn't aggressive in any way, but I remember hearing it. I was taught that as a child, I was to be seen and not heard, I was to obey. If an adult wanted to touch me, in my mind, I had to obey. I can assure you I've had loads of therapy to unpack all this stuff.

I'm going to tell you that my parents did the best they could. We all do as parents. However, when Christianity is taught in the home, I believe it can be taught while at the same time teaching sex education and, if you are religious, God's viewpoint in relation to the ideal sexual situation. We also need to recognize that sex is happening outside of these parameters and provide some sort of understanding and education for those situations. Providing a safety net for those instances does **not** have to mean we condone, but it **does** mean we care about our children enough to make sure that if they find themselves in those situations, they are prepared. It means we must help them be emotionally and mentally ready and able to deal with the consequences, good or bad, that follow it. If they are not yet ready, they need to know we are here for them as a safe place, otherwise the cycle repeats itself, or is never dealt with. If you do not deal with uncomfortable sexual situations, molestation, or rape, it can manifest later in life as detachment, inability to connect with your partner, other physical difficulties in the bedroom, or irresponsible promiscuity- and those are the best cases scenarios. In some instances, self-harm and/or suicide are the only escapes people who are not able to find help, feel they have.

To this day I detest milk. I detest the idea of farm life. I can appreciate the beauty of the country, from afar, but I cannot imagine ever stepping on a cow farm intentionally, it's ruined for me. Dairy milk makes me feel sick, although I'm probably lactose intolerant as well. Who knows the depth and reach this incident had in my life. My guess would be that it was quite significant. I did not realize until adulthood that every single instance of abuse rips away one's ability to self-protect, one's self-worth, and contributes to anger, which shows up immediately or manifests later in life.

The Girl & the Frying Pan

Circa 1980, Aurora, Minnesota had a population of around 2,600. That meant we rode bike safely everywhere, we didn't come home until late, everyone's yard was your yard, and the grocery lady knew your name. We had a modest rambler on a rather spacious yard in town. The backyard was full of green grass and occasionally dandelions, my mother's garden, and a clothesline. There was a line of trees that ran along the back of our yard to section it off from the neighbors. Our front yard was on an often-times used street, but I wouldn't call it busy. We had a few nice birch trees out front, along with a blue spruce, and a wide driveway. Our neighbors knew us, and we knew them, it had a really nice *Leave it to Beaver* feel.

On occasion, my mom would run to the store, which was probably a four-minute drive down some residential streets if she went to Potocnik's Grocery. If she went to the bigger store, Zup's, it was an eight-minute drive. When she would "run to pick something up quick," she would leave me at home with my older brother Aaron. Aaron and I were not particularly close. To this day, I don't know if it's because I'm adopted or because he just didn't like a little sister being brought into his world or what. He was four years older than me, and I'm sure I was a bother. Also, I was naughty, so I was constantly getting spanked or getting in trouble, and he probably thought I was a pain in the ass. In any case, there I was, left alone with my big brother.

Some of the neighborhood kids were playing outside as well. One kid was Aaron's friend, I can't recall whom, but whatever, that's not important. What ***was*** important, is that I had recorded myself singing on a little black tape recorder, and I thought it sounded pretty good! I sang, "Tomorrow" from the musical *Annie*, and I made sure to include obnoxious vibrato mixed in the notes for effect. Well, as my luck would have it and unbeknownst to me, Aaron and his friend were listening outside my door, laughing quietly. After I had come out of my room, I went outside and played with the sister of the friend he had over. Suddenly, out of the house comes Aaron, wielding the black tape recorder. He was laughing and threatened to play the tape I had made of myself singing. I was mortified.

"***Stop***!" I screamed, but he and his friend just laughed and ran in the yard with it. Clearly, he wasn't going to stop. I was physically unafraid of nothing when it came to my brother. I ran inside the house, grabbed a cast iron frying griddle, and proceeded to run after him with the goal of clobbering him over the head. It did not matter to me if it knocked him out cold, he could ***not*** play that tape! People would laugh at my attempts at bedroom music stardom! Oh my God, I would absolutely die! I was fast, and soon I was at his heels, and that's when my mom pulled into the driveway. Aaron acted like I was going to kill him, (I was) and I got in trouble. He didn't get in trouble for trying to humiliate me, but of course, I got to come in and sit and think about my actions.

This was not the only time I attempted to maim my brother with a spur of the moment weapon. Another time, we were downstairs in the family room, and I do believe he caught me in a little white lie. The jerk told on me, and I seethed with resentment. I was little for crying out loud! What did he care if I told a tiny lie? Why was **he** so perfect? I would show him! I grabbed a dart from the nearby dartboard and zipped it in his direction. Being the Robin Hood I fancied myself, I got him in the knee! Woohoo! He acted like an absolute baby about it, and of course, not only did I get in trouble for my little white lie, but I ***really*** got in trouble for throwing a dart at him. It's not like I hit him in the ***eye*** or the face or even the heart! I got his knee, and as far as I know, today he walks just fine and doesn't have any left-over chronic pain from it, or even a limp!

Interestingly, as much as I loathed my brother, I also wanted him to like me. He was a conundrum for me then, and even now, as he is an interesting person and difficult to really figure out. For instance, we were home alone, and I was downstairs playing in my playroom. I had a little kitchen in there and who knows what I was cooking up. Anyway, I could hear the radio turn on upstairs, and there was **rock** music playing! Ok, I told you, we grew up in a very strict home, and rock music was not allowed. The radio wasn't really allowed, only Christian tapes and Christian music and maybe a few instrumental records. So, with mom at the store, Aaron took advantage of the time to play a bit of the Devil's music. He was playing it softly, maybe so I wouldn't hear, but I heard. Oh, I heard. This was perfect! Perfect time for **me** to catch **him** in a lie! I could tell on him and finally watch **him** get in trouble!

I crept up the stairs as quietly as I could, knowing which ones creaked and which ones didn't. Step by step, holding my breath and moving like a jungle cat, I advanced on those steps one by one, grinning like a maniac. I was gonna get him good! I reached the top of the stairs, which opened to the kitchen. Once you opened the door, the stove was to your left, which was the perfect hiding spot. I could hide behind the side of the stove, and peer around the front of it, where I would have a crystal-clear view of the part of the living room that held the stereo. I could barely contain my excitement as I slowly peeked around the stove. I would not be disappointed. To my delight and surprise, there was my quiet, inconspicuous brother, in front of the stereo, dancing to "I Love a Rainy Night" by Eddie Rabbitt. He was doing the typical 80's style dance, snapping his fingers and going from one foot to the other, and I stared in utter shock. Even back then, I knew I was witnessing a human just enjoying a moment, and dammit, I couldn't bring myself to ruin it. I slowly retreated, creeping back down the stairs as carefully as I had crept up them. Once safely back in my playroom, I continued to smile to myself and somehow felt happy. I never told on him for listening to Satan's music, instead, I just logged it away for a happy memory.

On another occasion, I once again was left with my brother; now mind you, I was rarely left at home with my brother, but somehow the times I was, make for good fodder. This time, there was a thunderstorm, and I was afraid. It was loud and scary, and I wanted my mom to come home. I was watching out of the dining room bay window, holding the sheer curtains aside in an effort to will her home faster. I don't know how Aaron knew I was scared, I may have been crying, I may have told him, I don't really remember. What I **do** know, is that as I was looking out the window for my mom, there was Aaron (a.k.a. Patrick Swayze) by my side.

"Don't worry," he said, matter-of-factly. "The thunderstorm makes the grass really green. You might even see a rainbow." And just like that, I was shocked out of my terror. I looked at him like he was an alien, because he was never this nice to me. He was never outright **mean**, but he never was this nice. Those words made me see storms differently from then on, and I don't recall ever feeling scared of thunderstorms after that.

I tell you these little memories of my brother to kind of give you an idea of our relationship as we grew up. It was always like this, him not really seeing me, acting as if I didn't matter. Just when I was about to decide I hated him, he would do something kind, and I'd question my feelings all over again. I think this played into my insecurities of being adopted, and I wonder if I may have read into this a bit more than necessary, but probably not.

When I was a teenager, we lived at the Lakehouse by then, and Aaron had a group of his friends over for waterskiing and sauna. My parents liked Aaron's friends- they were always at our house. They truly a good bunch of guys, Mom and Dad genuinely enjoyed them. This was all happening during the "summer in my room," which I'll explain in a later chapter. For the purposes of **this** chapter, I will just sum up by saying that this was during a time I was very, very lost in the great big world. I had alienated myself from friends at school, and from any friends I may have had left at church. I had no one really, my best friend had stolen my boyfriend not too much earlier, and I was not getting along with my parents.

On this one early evening, after my brother and his friends had wrapped up a day of skiing and sauna, I believe they were going to a friend's cabin on the same lake as ours. I knew they were probably going to go drink and party, who knows if my parents suspected anything from my perfect brother, but I wasn't stupid. I could hear them all getting their things together and my parents telling them to have fun. "*Uh-huh,*" I thought bitterly. Aaron was like Ferris Bueller, but certainly not as cool. On the way up the driveway, I overheard their conversation.

"Maybe we should invite your sister," one of my favorite friends of his suggested. My eyes grew wide from my watch place in the house. I wanted to go!

"No," Aaron said, with a hint of disgust.

"Ok," continued the friend, "just asking." In that moment, I felt very rejected. Now I realize to the average reader with siblings, this may seem like nothing, but to a girl who felt abandoned and rejected her whole life due to being adopted, these slights were a big deal and hit me in all my sore spots. This wasn't the first time Aaron rejected the idea of me being around him or his friends, and I took it like an arrow right to the heart.

From that day forward, I made it my mission to at least make out with as many of Aaron's friends as I could. I knew it would piss him off if he found out, and it was the only thing I could think of to get my quiet revenge. So, one by one, my little hussy personality taking over, I divided and conquered. Some of the boys were surprised, but receptive. Here was their friend's "little sister" who wasn't so little anymore, pulling out moves that they didn't know I had. The truth is, when you're introduced to sex from way too early an age, you are not afraid of it, and you are even **good** at all things that include any form of physicality. At this point in my life, sex- and anything sexual was merely a means to an end, I didn't think about it being a big deal at all. No, I didn't have sex with all of Aaron's friends, but I kissed more than a few, and made out heavily with two of them. Deep down, I smiled to myself because now I was certain, that whenever they would come over to see Aaron, there I would be, and it would be ***our*** thing and Aaron would be none-the-wiser. Mr. "I'm So Perfect" would look like a fool, and I instantly felt better about things. *Take that,* **brother**. *Don't ever underestimate your sister, because I'll be one step ahead of you*, I thought.

In the meantime, I would grow up with Aaron and never really get to know him. I often wondered as a child what it felt like to have siblings that I was very close with, the kind that were your ride or die. Back in the Aurora house, there was one time I stood up for my brother. Jimmy Rennard, who was my brother's age, was the bully of our neighborhood. One late summer day, he was in our back yard, and he was picking on my brother. I was not having it. There he was, four years older than me, bigger than both me and my brother. I still remember his red plaid shirt and his dirty-blond hair. He was athletic and had a facial expression that seemed so mean! Yet, here I came, like David running at Jimmy's Goliath, and low and behold, I don't know if it was the impact of my full run, or the total shock of my audacity, but down he went! I proceeded to try and get a good position that would allow me to start pummeling him, but here came my mother to ruin the fun. I don't remember too much of what happened next, but I do know that I don't recall seeing Jimmy much after that. I don't know whatever happened to him.

So, Aaron and I just kind of went through childhood together and apart. Having moments in between where we were aware of each other, and even interacted when forced. He was not someone I could come to about anything, but like I said, he wasn't mean to me. He was not unkind. He was just indifferent, and for me, that was somehow worse.

The Girl & the Frog

I have always had a thing about not being able to escape. I suppose many people do. In just about every situation, my whole life, I've usually had a plan of escape, or a plan B as some people call it. It's been exhausting, but it's a survival mechanism. It's the way I've learned to deal with things so that I'm no longer in any situation where someone can take advantage of me. (Thanks abusers!) I even jumped out of a window on a date once because I panicked; that's a whole other story. You'll hear about that later in this book. Anyway, the point is, I've had things happen in my life that have made me plot all my get-aways in whatever situation. The following is one scenario I could have used an escape plan for:

One summer day, I was at a crush's house with my best friend Amanda. We were friends then, and still are, (albeit not as close) and of course I've forgiven her for stealing my boyfriend in 8th grade. As it turns out, he would not be my type now as the current me and my personality would probably eat him alive, but I digress.

Let's get back to the story. We were visiting friends of the family, and they had a boy my age who was, in my eyes, super dreamy. He had blond hair and blue eyes, and beautiful bone structure. I was only going into 7th grade, but I already knew what beautiful bone structure was, because I didn't have it. We'll call this boy Jesse, and he had lips that just made me want to kiss them. I was busy trying to get him to like me, or at least notice me, and of course I felt that competitive thing best friends feel between them, because Amanda was prettier than me, and I didn't want him to like her instead.

We were outside, and they lived in the country. Thankfully they didn't live on a farm, but they did have grassy fields by their house, and it was tall. As we were running around their yard, my friend Amanda picked up a bullfrog. It was **enormous**, gargantuan really. It was emerald green and had the largest white belly ever. I didn't like amphibians. I wasn't necessarily scared of them; I just didn't like them. I said rather loudly, "Get that thing away from me," trying to act all delicate like a real girl, because maybe then Jesse would see me as a dainty girl and like me…

It didn't go as planned. Instead, I started to panic, and the more I panicked and screamed, the more Amanda chased me with the frog. I don't think she understood how intensely scared I was because I was also laugh-crying between screams. With tears blurring my eyes, I lost my footing and fell. Now I'm on the ground, with this bullfrog being held by its toes, dangling over my face as I rolled away in the grass trying to avoid it. If I sat up, I would smack my face into its belly, so my best option was to roll until I had a chance to stand up and run again. I was terrified that the frog on steroids would land on me, and finally, *finally* after what seemed like hours, she stopped teasing me. I got up, hair askew, my heart in my throat, and tears in my eyes. I proceeded to pretend it was no big deal, because I wasn't about to let Jesse see me get mad. After that, I associated frogs with a bit of a panicky response. I think if that had been the only instance for me with frogs, I wouldn't be as terrified of them as I am now.

Turns out, Jesse did hook up with me later when I was much older. In junior high, there was a kiss or two, and then in my 20's, there was a night spent at his house that he shared with a few other guys. Unfortunately, I was a bit tipsy and can't remember how delicious it might have been. I do remember a camera flashing at me at one point, and I'm pretty sure I ended up in "**The Book**," what an asshole. But I guess you need to kiss a few frogs before you find the prince, or so they say.

The Girl & the Highball

There are a couple chapters thrown in here to offset the mood of some of the chapters you just read. Comic relief- if you will. This story comes to you from Lake Esquagama, in Gilbert, Minnesota. My grandparents (my dad's parents) had a home on the golf course and belonged to the country club there. They were good people, hard-working and very proper, yet down to earth as well.

Grandpa was a war veteran and unfortunately, I didn't take full advantage of listening to his stories. I now wish I had, and that I had asked him so much more than I did. Ah hindsight… Anyway, Grandpa was amazing. He wore golf attire much of the time. He had these polyester plaid pants in all different colors and patterns. He had solid polyester shirts he wore with them, and he always pulled his pants up high on his waist. At times, he wore white shoes to complete the look. Grandpa smoked a pipe now and then, and I loved the smell of sweet tobacco wafting through the house. He smoked cigars as well, and he enjoyed a good Jack and Ginger. They always had 7Up or Ginger Ale at their house, and to this day, those are my two favorite sodas.

Grandpa was one of the smartest people I knew. He was always reading something. He knew so much about so much. He ran a successful business, and he was a good provider and protector of Grandma. Back then, that was the way. He worked hard and he invested well. He had a small oil business, and a good work ethic. I looked up to him in many ways.

Grandpa and Grandma always had company. Whether it was family or friends, it was rare when you found them home alone. They had friends from everywhere, it seemed. On top of being excellent hosts, their house permanently smelled so good. I'm not sure if that was from Grandma's cooking, or peanuts and brandy and Grandpa's pipe. Grandma was an amazing cook, and there was never anything she made that I didn't like, oh- except pickled beets. They seemed to find their way to the table at every gathering.

When I was very little, I would love visits to their house when they lived in a little area of Virginia called Midway. Their home was on the top of Vermilion Drive, and I loved that house. You could look out the bedroom window and see all of Virginia in the distance. The midway house was big, and in my mind's eye, it was epic. Grandpa and Grandma always had enough room for all the family to visit.

It was difficult when they sold that house and moved to Gilbert. I never really liked the change of the things that brought me safety and security when I was a child, so I saw this as a real bummer. The Gilbert house was also very nice, as it was situated on Lake Esquagama and by the 7th hole of the golf course. It was a rambler, and they added an addition for more living and entertaining space. This was perfect for them since, like I said, they always had company.

On one occasion when they had many guests, I came out to visit them. I was 21or 22, I can't remember how old I was at this time. Grandpa knew I was of age, and he greeted me at the door like the gentleman he was.

"Hi Grandpa!" I said cheerfully, coming up the walk. On this visit, for the first time ever, Grandpa asked me a question I definitely was not prepared for.

He stood larger than life at the entry of the door, a smile on his face, looking at me through big, thick rimmed glasses. "Hi Sara, can I get you anything? A highball?"

I looked at him as if he were an alien. I was confused.

"An **eyeball**?" I asked, a little too shrill.

He kind of took a step back and looked at me through squinted eyes and a small ironic smile. I'm guessing he immediately regretted the offer. He kind of chuckled and repeated, "A **high**ball."

My brain thankfully made the correct connections, and I understood now that he was offering me a drink. Embarrassed at my blunder, I mumbled, "Er, no... thanks though". I figured if I couldn't recognize the word for an adult beverage, I probably shouldn't have one, at least not in front of Grandpa. Although I wanted a drink badly, (which I always do when I'm around family) I fucked that up now. I would have to wait until the next time and hope he re-offered.

Turns out, he didn't have to offer because the next time I visited Grandma and Grandpa, I helped myself. Thankfully, they were busy with their company, and I think my shenanigans went unnoticed. Either way, I had lots of fun memories at their home- highballs and eyeballs not-withstanding.

6

The Girl & the Reunions

Being adopted had such an impact on my life *in every possible way* that you can imagine. I've already briefly discussed the impact in my school life, being the only brown girl in my school was tough! At the time, in Northern Minnesota, it seemed like almost everyone was Finnish. If you weren't Finnish, you were probably Swedish or Norwegian or German, something white. No one was Mexican, Cuban, and Spanish like me. I stuck out like a sore thumb everywhere I went. Like I stated earlier, my adoptive mom is Mexican, but her experience was decidedly different from mine because she was an adult, she was not adopted, and she married into the Morgan family. I wasn't even **born** into the Morgan family as a half-breed. Instead, I was taken in as the orphan who needed a home, and I didn't look like anybody. This was never as apparent as when we would attend family reunions or the like.

Oh, I hated family reunions. I was well-aware that in fact, these people were not my ***real*** family. Pause for a minute. I am going to share with you that ***not one person*** in the Morgan family ***ever*** made me feel like I didn't belong. Not one person made a comment that could be considered excluding in nature. Everyone in the Morgan family loved me and showed me the same treatment that they showed other family members. What made me feel excluded was my own knowledge of my background, along with the color of my skin. If you go to a Morgan family reunion, you'll be swimming in a sea of blonde hair and blue or green eyes. Along comes Sara Morgan, with her dark skin and her jet-black hair and her eyes so dark, that later in life, a guy that was destined to become my ex used to call me "shark eyes" - fun.

Anyway, I rarely went to family reunions once I got older, but when I was little, I had no choice. Morgan family reunions were probably like many Northern Minnesota family reunions. They usually were at someone's lake home or cabin, and consisted of casseroles, Jell-O with whipped cream topping, Chex mix, veggie trays, fruit salads and chips. Grandma used to make a highly delicious Waldorf salad and a chicken casserole that were always crowd pleasers.

Sometimes Grandma would take out a letter from a relative in Norway, written in Norwegian, and would share it with other family members. Grown-ups would laugh with the little kids and tell them how big they'd gotten and all the things that you're supposed to say to kids to make them feel special and important. Our family reunions were always an affair that was nice and "proper." No one ever really got tipsy except my uncle, and sometimes my grandparents, and as an adult, I now get why they liked to indulge, or needed to indulge.

It was at one such reunion of sorts, that I dipped into the Jack Daniels in my grandpa's bar downstairs. I've always loved basements with bars. They looked so distinguished and there was a smell that was a mix of old basement, brandy, wood, leather, and something else. My grandparent's "something else" scent was cleaner, I think. My grandparents had a clean home, and it was never cluttered or messy or smelled bad.

The main floor of my grandparent's home was occupied with family, all making the typical conversation you hear at family reunions. There was croquet on the lawn in the back, drinks and food in the kitchen, and laughter coming from the family room. My fiancé Jackson and I found ourselves wandering down to their basement where I did a quick scan of the bar and found the Jack. BINGO! I quickly retrieved two of what I now know to be highball glasses from under the bar and poured us two Jacks on ice. They went down way too quickly, so I poured two more. Pretty soon, we had just about cut that bottle in half between the two of us.

What a couple of jerks, I think in hindsight. At the time though, it was my saving grace. Who wanted to face all the people in the family who weren't really my family **sober**? It was not fun to sit around and see the physical similarities between everyone but me. I always felt like I had highjacked the name "Morgan" and was a bit of an imposter.

We ended up leaving my grandparents' early: me, full on drunk, and my fiancé, who had to have had at least a little buzz. I remember giggling my way outside and my fiancé smiling to himself as he watched me trip up the grass to the little road. I decided after that, that the best thing to do would be counseling. No, I'm kidding. I decided the best thing to do would be to stop going to family reunions. It was evident I had some trouble with them.

The Girl & the Lost Week

We were living in Aurora, and I was about 14 years old, maybe 13. Our church school had long since closed, and I was now going to public school. My parents decided they needed a vacation, and my brother and I would not be going. Can't say I blame them. However, on this occasion, we would be staying home alone. My brother had to have been 18, he had to have been, but now as I think about it, maybe he was 17. He was still in school, I think. Anyway, my parents were going out of the country and had arranged for my aunt to call and check in on us from time to time while they were gone. I still can't believe they left us alone while they left the country, but I was a Generation X kid, so I suppose this makes sense.

While they were frolicking in Venezuela, I was flailing in Minnesota. I have no real recollection of that week. I came away from that week with spotty memories, very spotty. I have flashbacks of moments in time, but nothing to connect moment to moment. There's me going downstairs in an unfamiliar home. There's me turning onto a dark street. There's me running in the darkness in full panic. There's me being grabbed. There's me being shoved down by more than one person. There's me begging. There's me floating above myself and wondering where I am and how I got there. There's me realizing I have no real friends, no one who cares that I left that unfamiliar house by myself. There's me back at home, sitting in my room, gulping down bile. A day or two later, there's me waking up because mom and dad are back. There's me feeling anger and sadness and something else… shame? There's me, **knowing** I'm no longer a virgin, but either refusing or being unable to recall **how** I know that; there's only the knowing. There's me feeling the absolute sickness that comes with feeling like I'll never be safe or ok again.

After my parents returned home, we sat in the living room, and they pulled out gifts they brought back for us. I looked at my mom, all tanned and happy. I wanted to smack her. I hated her giddiness and excitement. I loved the gray shoes they brought for me, they were handmade and suede and so pretty; but at what cost? I felt abandoned, thrown out, forgotten. I had been a daddy's girl growing up, but now, I was startled with the realization of that feeling being gone; what had happened to me snatched that away. I hated that my mom and dad went on vacation and just left me with a brother I barely knew, and I decided that it was my mom's doing. I see now that my thinking was unfair, my mother is a wonderful woman. I just had no outlet for my intense anger. Mothers often-times unjustly end up bearing the brunt of the family's hurtful moments.

I didn't know then that I was already dealing with abandonment issues as the result of being adopted. I was adopted at 5 months of age, and during the previous 5 months, I went back and forth between my foster home and the hospital because I was sick with pyloric spasms. Obviously, I cannot remember any of that, but I **can** imagine what it could be like for an infant to cry endlessly, and not be picked up or given mother love. I don't know what my foster environment was like, but what I can say is that I've always relied on myself for as long as I can remember. When anything was wrong, I dealt with it myself, I preferred it that way. I **still** prefer it that way. I am told that I spent so much time in the hospital, that the attending physician wanted to adopt me. For some children, and it turns out, specifically me, this environment in my infancy created the perfect storm for abandonment issues. If my parents left me with a sitter or with my grandparents, I took it very personally. How could I not, given my predisposition to being left?

After that, I suppose the week I couldn't account for and the anger and resentment I felt toward my parents, particularly my mom, began to shape the next few years of my life. I began to resent them in full force, and, not knowing how to deal with the obvious trauma that happened while they were gone— trauma that was now piling on top of the trauma I experienced as a little girl, I started my descent into reckless thoughts and living. This was the turning point in my life that I could not come back from.

It would be years before I tell my mom and dad what happened while they were whooping it up in Venezuela. I was barely able to relay much of what happened, the events I could remember were just available to me in bits and pieces; the rest of the things were merely blank moments in my mind. I wouldn't have even told them about it at all, but someone I had confided in, told ***their*** parents, and their parents told my parents.

You see, I grew up like I said, in a home where I was loved and nurtured, but there was the intense fear of discipline for your actions. How on earth could I tell my parents about the many violations to my body and physical boundaries up until that point? Hell, as a child, I wasn't even ***allowed*** to have my own boundaries! I was afraid I would be in trouble, and since my parents never talked to me about sex in a way that was less religious and more human, the thought of them doing so now while I was already a teenager was mortifying. I was sure I was such a let-down as a child, and they probably regretted adopting me. Here was another reason I was different. Maybe this was happening to me ***because*** I was adopted. Maybe I was brown because I was destined to be dirty.

When girls sit around at sleepovers or in the school cafeteria and talk about this boy and that boy, every now and then, they ask if you're still a virgin. And if you're ***not*** a virgin, who did the deed? I was paranoid about how to answer that question because I had no answers. I couldn't think, and if I tried to think about it, my brain put the ***immediate*** brakes on, so much so, that I'm surprised I didn't have smoke coming from my ears. I had no clue, and who doesn't know who took their virginity? In the end, because of my not knowing the answer to this question, I made something up. I gave credit for my deflowering to a boy I barely knew and who I was sure no one else would know. As long as I had a name, any name, girls didn't pry too much. That's the thing about teenage girls: they want the info but don't care about the details or anything else about how you're feeling. Bitches, all.

Sometimes, I just hated everyone.

Over the years, I went to therapy to try and deal with these issues. Therapy goes ok, until I get to this part in my story. This part was usually the part where I would start missing therapy appointments and would decide I was doing just fine without help.

8

The Girl & the Condom

I was 15, just about to turn 16. We were living at the Lakehouse by now. I was happy because I was getting to go to Duluth school shopping with my boyfriend Matt and his friends. It would be just us, no grown-ups. I don't know how I swung that, but I did. We piled in the car that one of his friends drove, and we headed out of Virginia, Minnesota for the big city of Duluth. This was very exciting because getting off the Iron Range was always a win; we teenagers cherished the times we could escape. This day was one of those days.

The Duluth mall was gigantic compared to our little mall up north with its limited stores. Some of the spaces in the Virginia mall were vacant even, so that contributed to the feeling of boredom. I spent a good part of the day happily walking with Matt, who was tall and kind of handsome in that goofy way that only some boys get away with. He held my hand, and I was in Heaven. I liked him so much, but all we had ever done up until this point was kiss. God he was a good kisser. He had these lips that were full and reddish, and he had freckles. I've always liked freckles. Looking back, I guess you could say he was my first love.

The year before, he and I were kind of an item. At least, everyone in our church youth group knew and my best friend at the time, Amanda, knew as well. I usually only got to see Matt at church Sunday mornings, Sunday evenings, and Wednesday evenings. It may seem like a lot, but there was no real time alone, and if we somehow managed to be alone, some adult at church would find us and dutifully send us back to where there was a crowd. It seemed adults at that church were always taking it upon themselves to be on teenage paw patrol, as in "keep your paws off each other" patrol. I sometimes wonder if they were more preoccupied with the idea of sex than we were.

Anyway, the previous year, the summer I had turned 15, Matt stepped out on me with my friend Amanda. Yup, the same Amanda that held the frog over my head. I found out at summer camp, and I was furious. It only reiterated to me that I was an ugly, brown girl with no one of her own. Amanda was blue-eyed, and blonde-haired, and she had a beautiful face. Of course, he left me when she gave him the opportunity. Even though I was almost certain they didn't have sex, I didn't speak to her for an entire summer, betrayed as I was. Turns out, they didn't last, and by the following year, I had forgiven him.

So now here we were, school shopping together. At the time, brown leather jackets were the coolest item of clothing one could possess, and I talked him into one. He looked so good in it. I also talked him into a few sweaters. Matt was on the swim team at his school, and because of that, he had a trim waist and very broad, rounded shoulders. His shoulders were one of my favorite things about him, along with the way his jeans just sat on his hips and the six pack was visible when he would stretch or put his arms through his jacket.

When it was time to leave, we climbed in the car- Matt and I in the back seat with one other person. We cuddled under that leather jacket he bought and kissed on and off the whole way home. Looking back that must have been so uncomfortable for whoever was with us, but at the time, we didn't care. Horny teenagers seem to care about nothing but themselves. We ended up stopping at a rest stop on the way home because someone had to use the bathroom. We all went in and took the opportunity to do the same. The boys came out of the bathrooms laughing, but I thought nothing of it. They were always being stupid.

I was brought all the way home by Matt, and I was feeling delightfully blissful walking in the door. I was given so many kisses, my head was spinning. I had just spent the day with no parental supervision for almost 8 straight hours. It was glorious. I went in my room and avoided my parents for a bit while I changed into something comfy. I came out, and I believe we were going to eat or something, when the phone rang. Whatever, people called all the time, so I just hoped my dad would hurry up and get off the phone so we could eat. As it turns out, he got off the phone, talked with my mom, and then they both called me into their bedroom.

I swallowed back a lump in my throat, what could I have possibly done? I knew this wasn't good, because they both looked pretty serious, and I knew I was about to get the Spanish Inquisition about something. I came in and looked from one of their faces to the other.

"What?" I asked.

"We just got a phone call." I can't even remember which one of them said it. I shrugged- my shoulders frozen in the up position as I waited.

"From Matt's mom," they continued. My shoulders lowered into normal position, and I raised my eyebrows.

"Ok," I said, and made it sound more like a question.

"She found a condom in Matt's bag," they said in an accusatory manner, still standing, hands on their hips, looking at me.

A light bulb went off in my head. **That's** what they were laughing about in the bathroom, I remembered then. They bought the condom for a joke; he was supposed to find it when he got home but somehow, he saw it when they tried sneaking it in his bag. We weren't even *thinking* about having sex. Or at least, I wasn't. I suppose he was because he was a horny teenage boy, but we hadn't ever talked about it, and he never pushed the idea on me at all.

Almost with relief, I tried explaining the situation to my parents. "Guys, that was meant to be a *joke*. The guys bought it out of a *vending* machine in the *bathroom* on the way home to give Matt grief… Isn't that funny? A *vending* machine that sells condoms! It wasn't serious." (At the time, vending machines that sold condoms were kind of a new thing in the area we lived in.)

But when I looked at them, I could see that for some reason, this *was* serious. Seriously? Furthermore, how was this *my* problem? Why did Matt's mom call *my* parents? Shouldn't she be lecturing her own kid? How did I get involved? It took a lot of convincing on my part, and I'm still not sure they believed a word I said, but I was actually telling the truth. Also, how embarrassing to think your *dad* thinks you're having sex! God it was the worst when my mom told him I got my period, and he came in my room and said something along the lines of "you're a woman now." Holy shit, I was mad at my mom over that. In any case, I was again embarrassed and ashamed over something that first-of-all, is natural, and second, something I wasn't even doing, and third, if I ***was***, wasn't it a good thing if we were having safe sex?

So much for a decent night, I thought. Now things were awkward. If they got this mad over a condom, imagine how mad they would be if they knew the other things I'd done by now, and the things that had been done ***to*** me! This was another reason I kept my mouth shut, there was just no safe place.

As it turns out, they didn't need to worry about Matt's condom that year. It was much later, coincidentally when we were no longer an item, that he snuck me in his bedroom window, where he took out a condom, and for the first time, we had sex. It was tender, it was sweet, and it was innocent, free from abuse, free from force, free from anything other than the fact that he was going through things, I was going through things, and we ran away from those things, and towards each other. To this day he has a soft place in my heart, because I think a first love often does.

The Girl & the Minivan

By this time in my life, I'm doing a lot of sneaking around, and a decent amount of exploring my sexuality. Up until this point, most sexual advances toward me have been unwelcome, and then forced, whether gently or not. My self-esteem was at an all-time low, because when older males exert their power over you and take from you sexually, you feel used, dirty, no good, powerless to control your own destiny, ashamed, and then the self-loathing begins. When you self-loathe, there is no love to help you help yourself. This is where I was.

Now, I'm not going to say I was an innocent angel by any means, but we must establish that I had started a pattern of self-harm that was masquerading as sexual freedom, where I could call the shots. I fooled myself into thinking I was in control, and that it didn't matter what I did sexually, because that ship had sailed. Although I wasn't the captain at ***that*** time, I sure was now. I had a lot of nerve, and this chapter is about that.

Every time my parents got a new vehicle, it was a station wagon. They even had the wood-paneled kind! As time marched on, so did the style, and minivans were now in vogue with families. OMG it sucked. Could we never get a cool car? Ever? The only saving grace about the minivan was that the color was black and not beige. I hated opening the side door and stepping out of that beast. Alas, there was just nothing cool about it.

What I lacked in the "too cool for school" department, I made up with my looks that were starting to at least be more appealing, and coupled with my flirty nature, I could be quite intoxicating to the boys at my church. Our church had a sister church in Duluth, and I knew some of the kids from there. Somehow, I was able to be in contact with one boy from Duluth in particular. I'll call him Nate. He was cool, in that when there was a summer camp, or a church retreat, he would show up in the best clothes ever. He was relatively cute, and just carried himself differently than the other boys. He cared about fashion; he wore things the other boys were not confident enough to wear. He was a flirt, and right away he and Amanda hit it off. Yes, the Amanda with the bullfrog; the Amanda that stole my boyfriend yet was somehow still my friend. Anyway, they were kind of an item whenever he would come up north.

On this occasion, he and I had been talking. Just talking like friends mostly, and although there was a little flirting, it didn't seem like anything serious. Somehow, we decided to hang out. He was going to be home alone that night, I think maybe his mom worked. I waited until my parents went to bed and fell asleep, snuck out of the house, and went across the road to the garage.

Guys, you need to understand something here. I lived in Britt. Britt is 20 minutes north of Virginia. Duluth is at least an hour south of Virginia. I was basically an hour and 20 minutes away from Nate. Somehow, that didn't stop my boldness that was clearly out of control. I got in the black minivan, backed it out of the garage, and **started the drive to Duluth**! How fucking ballsy and stupid of me! I was lucky I didn't hit a deer or get pulled over.

I arrived in Duluth and somehow got a hold of Nate; I must have used a payphone because cell phones were not yet a thing. He gave me his address (thank God he was still awake) and I drove there feeling quite excited but also scared at the fact I drove here in the middle of the night. What if my parents woke up and checked on me for some reason? What if they saw I wasn't in my room? Would they check the garage? Would they report their car stolen? Would they be worried? Welp, it was too late now. I was in Duluth, and I was just now parking the minivan on the street where Nate lived.

Nate invited me in, and straight to his bedroom. The rest of his house was dark and quiet, no one was awake. Or maybe they weren't home, I don't know, and I didn't care. He was in sweats and a tee shirt, and I was suddenly aware of how soft his hair looked and how it curled in a few places. Sure enough, as soon as we were in his room and the door closed behind him, he kissed me. I was a bit surprised there was no talking beforehand, but I went along with it because it was **Nate**! One of the coolest kids at our summer camps was kissing **me**. He was an excellent kisser as well, and I smiled to myself as I thought, "Fuck you, Amanda. Fuck you for humiliating me with that frog years ago. Fuck you for taking my boyfriend last year. I'm going to take yours now." I was sure she hadn't done that with him because I knew they didn't really get any time together and she wasn't that type of person anyway. It was at this point I thought, *if you fuck me, I will fuck you back, only **worse***.

The deed itself was ... meh, mediocre I suppose. The kissing and everything else happened to be much better. He wasn't a generous lover by any means, I mean, he was a teenage boy so what did I expect. Afterward, we kissed and said goodbye, and I walked into the night to my parent's black minivan. I didn't feel great, I even felt a little bad; bad about myself and what I did just for acceptance and validation and even revenge. Who was I? Why was I like this?

I got back in the van and bee-lined it home. It was already coming up on daytime, and I was going to roll in **after** 6:30. I was terrified I wouldn't make it in time. I was also fighting my eyes feeling oh-so-tired; all I wanted to do was go to bed, but I couldn't **because I had school**! Yes, I had to go to school that morning. I drove home with the windows open and the radio blasting. What a fucking idiot I was! After I managed to get the minivan back in the garage, I rushed across the road and down my driveway. To my absolute horror, there was my dad in the kitchen window, running water to make a pot of coffee. Oh **FUCK**! I was so fucked. My once tired mind was now suddenly wide awake, scrambling around for an explanation that would be needed the moment I walked in the door. I couldn't sneak down the side of the house and come in the basement door because he would both hear me and see me when I came up the steps to the main floor. I would have to come in the front.

He looked up at the motion he must have sensed and saw me walking down the stairs outside toward the door. His eyes got wide as he took in his daughter fully dressed at about 7 in the morning, coming down from the circle driveway. I walked in, trying to look innocent.

"Well, Sara… good morning! What are you doing?" he asked, still holding the coffee pot mid-air in one hand.

"Hi, Dad," I made a show of wearily hanging up the car keys, slowly kicking off my shoes and dutifully hanging my head. "I didn't want to tell you, but… I failed a test at school. It's an important test. I was given permission to go in very early to re-take it, and so I did. I'm sorry. I took the car to go do that because I didn't want you to know I had such a bad grade."

I was impressed with my cleverness. Put a bit of guilty action or reason in the lie, make it sound like you're coming clean, and it sounds legit. Ok, I want you to know that my dad isn't stupid; but for whatever reason, he bought it. Maybe it was the fact that I was dressed appropriately and not in something sexy. Maybe it was the look of shame in my "bad grade" that I wore. Maybe he was just in a good mood or was distracted by other things. For whatever reason, he let it go, and I hurried upstairs to salvage whatever amount of time I had left to clean up and get ready for school. As I got ready, I looked at myself in the mirror and was scared at my audacity, my ability to do what I just did and come out unharmed.

The only saving grace in this whole story is that it was a bit of sweet revenge I suppose; I felt like the betrayal I suffered the previous year was now even, I could put it behind me. I smiled as I brushed my teeth. He **was** a good kisser- I'll give him that. Oh, and "fuck you, Amanda!"

The Girl & the California Boy

At our church, we had a winter retreat, and a spring retreat. Some churches may refer to them as lock-ins, but our church called them retreats. They were for the older kids: 9th grade and up maybe. They were usually a full long weekend, and they consisted of devotions, team time, games, outside play, great food, and so many other kids from surrounding areas. The Duluth kids would come, and sometimes the even **cooler** kids from the cities would show up. ("The Cities" is what northern Minnesotans refer to Minneapolis and St. Paul as: the "Twin Cities," or "Cities" for short.) The further away you lived from the Iron Range, the cooler we Iron Range kids thought you were.

This time, for the winter retreat, a group of kids came from our sister church in Duluth. I had known these boys from camp, kind of. I knew who they were and had seen them once or twice before, but this time was different. This time, they saw **me**. I was about 15 or 16, and right away, I noticed Jason Banks. He lived in California and spent time with his dad in Duluth every now and then. He was tall, with dark hair and dark eyes. He was older than me, and up until this point, I hadn't even thought he would look my way. Somehow, he did. I don't even know how it happened, but soon we were kind of flirting, and it was noticeable to the other girls that I had first dibs. In hindsight, I don't even know if they were even interested, probably they weren't.

At the time, I felt like I had hit the jackpot. Not only was I flirting with and getting the attention of an older boy, but he was not from the Range. Not only that, but he wasn't even from Minnesota! He was from California! Could it get any cooler? He ended up asking me out, and from then on, I was all in. We went to dinner with his parents later in the month, they took us to Pickwick in Duluth. This is the point where things really started to go downhill for me.

Jason was a dick, a **complete** dick. He didn't care about rules. I mean, *I* didn't care about rules, but he **really** didn't care about rules. He looked a bit like a pretty boy, and he was into weightlifting which was kind of hot at the time for me I suppose. He became such a puke later that I hate even writing this chapter. However, it is necessary because it's basically how my leaving home started.

Over the year, we were kind of an item. Yes, he was cool, and yes, I got to see him sometimes. He was going to college nearby because he wanted to go into a certain profession that one of the colleges on the Iron Range has a good program for. My parents did not like him or the idea of him. I suppose they saw how shifty he was, and his jerk potential was radiating off the charts. I only saw freedom and something different from what I was currently experiencing.

Jason listened to the coolest rap music, and he often talked about California. In addition, he slowly began to manipulate me. It started with little accusations of my unfaithfulness. It got to the point where I was doing everything he said to do. Sit in the snow naked to prove my loyalty? Yes, I'll do that. Show him I care about him by defying my parents and going to see him? Yes, I can do that. Start getting into weird sexual things to let him know I trusted him? Sure, I can do that.

One day, my dad went to see him at his apartment/dorm to set him straight. I wasn't there, but I know Jason used his size to try and intimidate my dad. For whatever reason, even this did not jar me into reality as I was already so engulfed in my own self-loathing, shame, and fear. I remember hating that Jason did that, and, also feeling like this wasn't even about me. It was a chance to defy authority, and it only made it better that my dad was his target. As a former "daddy's girl," this made my heart hurt a little, but I didn't know what to do- I was already in so deep. Finally, my parents had enough, and I'm pretty sure they threatened him with statutory rape, which would ruin his career and all his college would go down the drain. In the end, he moved back to California. We continued talking, either by mail or by me riding my bike five miles to the Britt Short Stop, where I would use the payphone to talk with him for long periods of time.

During the time while he was away, I was floundering in my predicament. I had no control over myself really. I had been molested many times, even raped by now, and it seemed to all come crashing down around me. I had no one to talk to, I was sure my parents would blame me for the things that happened. I couldn't talk about everything; I would die of shame and embarrassment first.

The California boy again became a hero since he was now living far away. He was an escape I could write to and imagine being with.

He wasn't here to hurt me or manipulate me, but he was available for someone to lean on and agree with me that my parents were not being fair, the world wasn't fair, and it was just the two of us against the whole unfair world.

My parents would go snooping through my room and find letters he or I wrote, and then they would confront me with it. Their snooping would only re-iterate to me that I couldn't trust them with my secrets. I would go wild with rebellion, yelling at them and saying hurtful things. The whole time I did this, in my mind I was really screaming, *why **me**? Why did these things happen to me? Why did men hurt me? Why was I just a thing they used and then threw away?* **WHO TOOK MY VIRGINITY?** But in the real world, I was just yelling and rebelling. My parents bore the brunt of my hurt and anger and feelings of abandonment. I felt like I was literally losing my mind. I began to question my sanity. I stopped eating for a while, it was the only thing I could control. I became very thin. I would spend hours in my room like a caged animal, needing to get out of this place called the Iron Range that by now held so many bad memories for me. I spent almost an entire summer in my room, emerging only to go to work.

I still had to somehow function and go to school, and I was forced to go to church. I was losing church friends because of my rebellion. The girls stopped wanting to be around me, and hurt by their exclusions and their judgment, I would retaliate by stealing boyfriends and being a major bitch. Oh, I noticed all the goings-on: the church girls would get together and not invite me, and it stung. I felt like I was on a trajectory of failure, excluded and alone. There were sleepovers at houses that did not include me, and I pretended it didn't hurt. I suppose they were afraid of getting involved with me, because by then, the rumors were starting that I was rebelling at home and giving my parents a lot of grief. How did these rumors even start? No one knew what was going on with me at home, I thought, so my parents must have confided in a friend or two. The rumors had to come from their friends then, as they probably gossiped to others. *Nice,* I thought, *fucking nice. No one is who they say they are, no one.*

I was completely wrapped up in the California boy, and I kept him close because he seemed to be the only one who I thought cared and at least made me feel like I was seen. He would listen to me, while others around me would demand answers. He would empathize with me, while those around me only wanted to judge me. And so, the year went by with me spinning out of control, out of touch, and out of my mind.

Previously, our church experienced some issues within itself. It had split, and the effects of that split seemed to go on and on. From what many of us teenagers could see, it was a bunch of adults fighting amongst themselves over who was a better Christian. There was more to it than that, of course, but for many, that's really what it boiled down to. On one occasion, a few members of the church generously said they would come over and show my parents the scriptures and where they were going wrong. I knew my crazy year and my rebellious blow-outs contributed to their opinions of my dad's ability to lead.

To those individuals that came over that day and raked my parents over the coals, I would say:

"You had **no idea** what we were dealing with in our home! My poor parents didn't know what was going on with me, as I couldn't tell them! I was being sexually abused, and as a result, I was going insane! My parents knew a **little** about it, but not everything. They were trying to help me, but because of my own traumatic beginnings and the road behind me, they could not help me. You individuals sat there and judged my parents, and all the while, my parents never betrayed my secrets to you to help you understand; because you lacked the capacity to show grace in the first place. My parents never betrayed my trust, even though doing so would maybe clear them of any inability to lead. So, chew on that, and I hope that you realize that although I forgive, I do not need to include you in my life. I've tried, but it proves to be too toxic for me."

The people who judged my family, what they did was cruel and arrogant, let it be known. And we are not done talking about the California boy. You'll read about him more later.

The Girl & the Football Player

Remember chapter four, The Girl and the Frog? Well, I had another incident that was the deciding factor that caused me to avoid walking on grass at all costs, especially barefoot.

This was the summer I turned 17, and I was doing everything I could to fit in and be liked. We had moved from Aurora to the worst place I could imagine as a kid, and that was Britt, Minnesota. I would have to change schools, live in a cabin that was like living in Swiss cheese, and endure that whole process for years.

We moved when I was going into 9th grade I believe. By 11th grade, I still hadn't broken out of the uncool group of kids I belonged to. Even though my friend Amanda went to my school and was pretty and popular, I just wasn't really accepted fully. I'm not sure why that was. It could have been my brownness, it could have been that I was projecting my insecure demeanor everywhere and kids picked up on that, it could have been that they were just assholes and didn't want to include me. I wasn't necessarily an outcast, but I wasn't popular, and I basically was a nobody. Sometimes they were nice and polite, but I could tell it wasn't like they genuinely ***wanted*** me there. By summer of my 11th grade, they started to accept me a little more.

Because it was summer, that meant Merritt Days was in full swing in the little town of Mt. Iron, Minnesota. Merritt Days was a festival that ran in late summer, and it was packed with everything you would expect a small-town festival to be packed with. They had bands, local of course, food vendors, small rides for the kiddos and, because it was the Iron Range area of Minnesota, there was lots of booze. The Iron Range is known for many things, and people who like to party is one of them. There was lots of food, a live band or two, and a parade; it was one big, happy gathering.

I attended this event with some friends, in fact, it was my birthday weekend! Absolutely we were drinking, not many adults in the area got too excited about underage drinking at Merritt Days. It was just how it was. I was coming up from the C group at school and being welcomed by the B group, so I for sure wasn't popular, but I wasn't a loser either like I had been. I suppose some of the boys started noticing me, but not all of them, and not the ones I wanted to notice me. Many of my classmates were at Merritt Days, and among them was a certain football player who was going out with an acquaintance of mine. He was one grade ahead of me, and even though I didn't really like him like that, I was pleased that he seemed to notice me that night. However, since I knew he was dating another girl, I didn't get too excited.

Toward the end of our night, thanks to a bit of booze, things got confusing, and I was separated from my group of friends. I tried to figure out how I was going to get back to wherever I was staying. I found myself walking along the edge of the field where some rides and attractions had been set up in honor of the festival, when this football player I mentioned earlier - I'll call him Josh, caught up with me and asked me where my friends were. I laughed and told him I had no idea, and I hoped I didn't sound nervous that one of the football players was really talking to me!

"Hey," he said huskily. Josh gently grabbed me and faced me to him, and I held my breath as he started kissing me. I kissed him back, because the need be accepted was way stronger than the knowledge of the other girl he was dating and the fact that I barely knew him. His breath reeked of alcohol, probably like mine did, but I didn't care. Pretty soon, he had sort of pushed me to the ground, firmly but still gently, and I found myself complying for the time being. But then, when he started making weird noises and getting a bit too handsy, I was aware of the fact that the panic I had become so familiar with, was setting in. I knew this change in men all too well. "The point of no return," I called it. The more I pushed his hands away, the more forceful he became.

It felt like all the alcohol I consumed that night was suddenly settling into my body, like NyQuil does when you take a large capful on an empty stomach, and it hits you about 5 minutes later. I felt as weak as a baby and my limbs felt heavy like giant stones. I noticed that I could barely speak.

"Stop it," I managed, but it came out like a whisper. He just seemed to be more excited by my struggle.

I couldn't shout, I felt like there was an elephant on my chest. I kept struggling as I felt the weight of him on top of me, and the more I struggled, the more he shushed me and held me down. I felt powerless to move; I felt like I was watching something happen in slow motion to someone else. Josh was pulling down my shorts, and as I weakly writhed underneath him to get away, I started worrying I would not be able to breathe, he seemed like dead weight. He kept tugging and pulling, until finally he got my shorts down around my calves, along with my underwear. By this time, I was in full panic mode, and I could no longer move. Almost as soon as the panic hit me full force, it started to go away; I became almost numb, even "airy" feeling, as I succumbed to my fate.

As one lonely tear slid down my cheek, I turned my head and looked over to my right, and there, sitting frozen in time, like me, was a frog. It was dark of course, and I could barely make it out against the tall grass I was laying in. Every now and then, it would blink, and the lights from the festival would make its eyes shine like crystals. For an instant, I thought it would hop my way, and I was sure I would pass out from being so terrified of it touching me or being next to me while Josh was by now moving in short little jerks inside of me. I felt sick, and for one brief moment, I feared I would throw up right there, but thankfully, I started feeling the fresh, cool summer air wash over me and the fogginess of my brain started to dissipate. Josh, now finished, was getting up, barely looking at me as he buttoned and zipped his jeans closed. I got up, and as I pulled myself together, I heard him say, "We're good, right?" I just stared back at him through vacant eyes as he started walking away, leaving me to try and figure out what to do.

I don't remember much of the rest of the night. I don't know where I went after that. I didn't tell anyone. I believed that if I told anyone, they would say I wanted it, because Josh was a football player, and I was a nobody. By the time I was 17 years of age, this is where my self-worth lay. I didn't dare tell my parents, because I was not supposed to be drinking at my age, or at any age, and I most definitely would be told that my choices played a role in what happened to me. I got myself into this situation, I was to blame. There would be no one to advocate for me, and I didn't know how to advocate for myself.

I had heard later that Josh and his girlfriend had broken up because he had cheated on her. It was with some other girl, and the girlfriend had found out. I recall hearing her talk about it later, and I thought she was so much better off without him, because he was a puke. I couldn't bring myself to tell her, because it didn't really matter, did it. It was done, over with. You couldn't un-ring that bell. It didn't occur to me that perhaps if I had been able to speak up, maybe I could have helped prevent him from doing that to someone else. What **did** occur to me, was that Josh, in fact, was a rapist, and I was no more the captain of my own ship.

It also occurred to me that I was now utterly terrified of frogs. It wasn't just that I couldn't stand them, I was truly scared of them. They sat there watching the world through their blinking eyes. They saw everything evil, and they hopped along to finish the rest of their evening, croaking by the nearest pond. And if you see that much evil, then you become evil by proxy, don't you?

The Girl Goes Bananas

By this time in my story, I'm probably one shrink visit away from being diagnosed as certifiably nuts. I was completely out of control, and it was not good. I was still writing to California boy. I was locking myself in my room and avoiding family. I felt like I wanted to legit murder my parents, I was so mad at them. At the time, I couldn't even say **why** I was so mad at them, and the answer to that question was only clear recently in deep therapy all these years later. I had been mad at them because they couldn't help me. If your parents can't help you, who can? I was upset because the tools they possessed with which to help me, didn't work for me. It was like trying to fix a clock with a jackhammer, a wrench, and a backhoe. What I needed required more intricate tools, delicate tools, more modern tools. I was so frustrated, and the fact that they loved me only made it harder. It added to the guilt I felt for being angry. I was feeling angry at someone who was truly doing their best, although back then, I didn't understand any of this.

Furthermore, I needed to be free of the area I lived in. Every visit to town made me want to throw up. Every country road made me sick to my stomach. Every car ride made me feel woozy. Now I know these emotions were triggered by flashbacks, familiar smells and sights related to places and people who had abused me. Milk made my stomach churn. Looking at a particular family made my blood boil. Football players and football cheerleaders made me seethe with wrath. Seeing the girls at church who ignored me and didn't give a shit about the real me, made me want to scream. Seeing adults' knowing, judging looks made me feel defensive and angry. Being so stifled in the country in my room made me feel panicked.

My parents had me stay with my grandparents for a week or so, to help bring down the intensity of the situation. I loved the time with my grandparents, and it hurt me to see their genuine concern written across their faces. I disliked hurting them, and I tried to be on my best behavior.

Grandma even borrowed my fuchsia-colored silk shirt to wear to bridge one day, which made me feel proud. When she returned from bridge with the ladies who lunched, she told me a funny little story. Their bridge game was held at the Holiday Inn, poolside, and when she got up to go use the bathroom, she fell in the pool! My pink silk shirt had gone in the water, and Grandma felt awful about it. I assured her that it was just fine, and we kind of had a giggle together over it. I did lose some of the brightness of the shirt, but that was fine. It just felt so good to laugh, truly laugh.

I couldn't stay at my grandparent's forever, though, and soon I was back at home, and the tumultuous exchange of interaction began again. My parents were trying to control me, to get a handle on my behavior. That was probably the worst thing they could have done. Unbeknownst to them, what I was going through didn't need absolute control, it needed someone to just be able to meet me where I was, with a soft approach and a gentle lead. I was like a wild dog, and while some may try and tame with a heavy hand, others realize that trust needs to be established first.

Because things were so out of control, I even ended up in the Kinney shelter, where the "bad" kids go. A car ride resulted with me in the back of a cop car, verbally insulting the police officers every mile of the journey. They took me to the shelter, where I was to stay to hopefully give everyone in my family a break from each other. No one knew what they were really dealing with because I would not talk about it. To my parent's credit, they **did** consider counseling for me, which was a big deal, because in our church, God was the solution to everything, not man. I would later argue that He gave us doctors to help us, so there's that.

The Kinney shelter was a home that kids stayed in for a few days or even weeks. You were basically given a bed, and there were group chores, group activities, strictly monitored bedtime, people on night duty walking around the home with flashlights making sure you weren't sneaking out… you get the picture. I both hated it and liked it. First off, I was a bit snobby (this was a defense mechanism, if people thought I was fabulous, maybe I was fabulous), so being in a shelter was bit humiliating. Second, I hated anyone trying to tell me what to do, they didn't know me. Third, I did welcome the moment to breathe and stop fighting with my parents constantly. Yet, I must not have enjoyed that part too much because I was planning my escape from the moment I arrived there.

One day, the rest of the kids at the shelter and I were being treated to a visit to the park. I don't care that I'm 17 and going to the park; *I'm not going to be stuck in that house any longer*, I thought. We all piled in the van, yes, the van (it probably had county numbers on the side and everything, how embarrassing) and we were driven to Virginia so we could go to the Olcott Park. I think we each had a bag lunch as well. I had struck up a friendship with a girl named Ellie, and although she was not some-one I could see myself being friends with on the outside, she was up for scheming on the inside, and that's what I needed. I couldn't do this myself or it might draw too much attention. It had to look like we were just two friends wandering a bit further off than the rest of the group, just two friends busy looking at flowers or chatting while walking along.

We agreed that we would leave the shelter during lunch on this field trip day. We would be in town, so it's not like we were in the country, far away from everyone. Kinney was 10 miles from the nearest town one way, and 11 miles the other town the opposite direction. Coming into Virginia was perfect. We were right in the middle of things, and our friends were nearby. I had no clue where I was going to go or what I was going to do for food or money, but I was going to leave. I didn't belong at the shelter. Somehow, in my warped mind, it was beneath me. I think now, it was me needing to escape from the confines of another situation that was out of my control. Control over my surroundings was becoming more important as time went on.

We started by walking and chatting, staying well within view of the rest of the group. It was a nice day and we just looked like two girls hanging out. Once we were as far away from the group as we thought was safe without being told to come back, we took off running. Ellie had plans to go somewhere, but I didn't really have a plan. I just wanted to get out of the situation I was in. So, I ran, glancing over my shoulder to see if they were going to run after me. Surprisingly, no one seemed to notice that we took off right away, so there was no yelling or chasing at all! A bit anticlimactic, but I would rather that than the alternative.

I found myself in the middle of Virginia, not sure where to go. I knew I couldn't stay in Virginia all night, where would I sleep? I decided I would call my friend Bill and see if he could give me a ride someplace; I didn't know where, but anywhere would do. Bill lived in Mt. Iron, which was only 5 minutes away. I told him the situation, and he agreed to pick me up. The catch was, he would only bring me home and nowhere else. At the time, I was annoyed. It seemed like Bill thought he was somehow better than me and I was embarrassed. Now that I'm older, I realize he didn't want to get in any trouble, and he must have figured that the best thing for himself and for me was to just bring me home.

Bill dropped me off, way out in Britt, without even asking for gas money. Maybe it was because that summer I had gone with him to his cabin a few times and we fooled around, a few times. Maybe it was because he had a soft heart and was a good guy. I don't know. For whatever reason, he didn't ask for gas money, and I didn't offer. Soon, there we were, going down the circle driveway of my home. I think my dad was outside and my mom was in the kitchen, or maybe it was the opposite, but the looks on their faces was priceless. They went from looks of total surprise, to relief that I was safe, (because by now I'm sure they had a phone call, and it was hours since I had left) and then I saw my mom's face rest with her lips in a thin line neither smiling nor frowning. She probably just realized that her peaceful week was now gone, and she would have to deal with me; that was no small task being how rebellious and bananas as I was acting. They thanked Bill, who seemed a little pleased with himself. I wanted to smack him, didn't tell them that he knew what I looked like with hardly anything on. But here he was, acting like the hero of the day. I just rolled my eyes instead and went into the house and up to my room.

After my parents saw that the Kinney shelter wasn't going to work, it was a whole different ball game. I would like to stress the fact that the truth of my now many episodes with sexual abuse was hitting me in full force, however, at the time I did not know this was happening. I thought I was just rebellious, just a bad kid. I knew on some level that the past was doing a number on me, but I didn't know to what degree. When I came home from the Kinney Shelter, I started seeing the seriousness and the deep affect abuse was having on me, and it scared me. I was like a caged animal, out of control and out of my mind. I just wanted to escape; escape my room, my house, my parents, the spotlight on me, the judging eyes of people I knew… and I think, escape myself. I hated myself, and my behavior, but I couldn't stop. My wounds took on a life all their own.

My home life was now so volatile, that finally, my parents called up the California boy, and told him, "She's all yours" or something along those lines. I am sure their safety was in question, as I had scratched my mom and I don't think they felt like the environment was safe from my anger and the uncertainty that went with my state of mind. I must have had a job that I was holding, I can't remember for sure, but I must have, because I had a little money. I bought myself a one-way ticket to San Francisco, and my parents agreed to drop me off at the airport in Minneapolis. I would live with the California boy - Jason and his mother and brother in a house in California. I would go to school and graduate there, and I couldn't be more excited because it meant I would get to flee where I was. I would soon leave my small-town environment, the land of ice and snow and mosquitos and humidity, and I would be in the land where winter never really arrives, and the sun glitters on every ocean horizon. I forgot about good ol' Shakespeare's observation that "all that glitters is not gold…"

13

The Girl Arrives

Yours truly was barely 17, and my clothes were packed. I didn't think anything of the fact that I was taking a suitcase of my parent's, it never crossed my mind until now. I was terribly excited to be leaving the Iron Range. I don't know how things worked out school-wise, what with the transferring of my transcripts and all of that. I don't know who took care of that. I'm assuming my parents did, and I vaguely remember something about a permission form they had to sign to allow me to leave their home and live across the country.

By this time, my former best friend Amanda and I were not really speaking all that much. It was evident at school that I had gone bananas, I was most definitely now considered a "rebel" and I was pretty sure our friendship embarrassed her at times. I remember it being painfully awkward between us the last weeks of school in Mt. Iron, but I couldn't worry about that. I had bigger fish to fry.

I decided for the flight, I would wear my black miniskirt, my fuchsia silk shirt (yes, the one that went in the pool along with my grandma), black nylons and my black heels. Hey, it was 1990 and I was trying to look grown up! I wanted to look good when I arrived in Cali. I couldn't believe I was really going, and I couldn't believe my parents were bringing me to the airport. It was very awkward, to say the least. I can't remember much about the drive at all. I just know that freedom from my situation was a few hours away. I think my parents may have felt some relief as well on their part, although I'm certain it was accompanied by great disappointment and gut-wrenching grief.

I boarded the plane all by myself, a teenager flying across the country to a brand-new life. I felt grown up and free, and I smiled as I walked to my seat. I felt so cosmopolitan, and if I could have gotten away with it, I would have ordered a cocktail just to complete the feeling. As it was, I sat in my seat and stared out the window. I felt so much excitement bubbling up inside me, and I think a bit of shock at my own guts. I looked around the plane and wondered if anyone knew that my life was going to take on a major change.

What would it be like, living with my boyfriend, his mom, and his brother? Would there be lots of rules? What would the days be like? What would the nights be like? Would people like me? At that thought, I remember feeling a surge of panic. I would be the new girl at school again, and since I was so used to sticking out like a sore thumb, I was worried that I would face that once more. Everyone would stare and I would be "the Mexican." *Oh well, nothing I haven't dealt with before*, I supposed. I crossed my legs like a grown-up woman, and as we took off, I smiled once again— goodbye, Minnesota.

The flight seemed to go on and on, but in truth, it was under 4 hours. My stomach started getting butterflies as we made our decent into San Francisco. I could see out the window that it was sunny, and I couldn't believe I was about to become a "California Girl." Stupidly, I quietly hummed "I wish they all could be California Girls" and then, realizing my corniness, I stopped and finished the tune in my mind only.

When we were at our gate, I nervously got up and joined the slow-moving line filtering out of the plane. I tried not to smile. I tried keeping it cool, but I was so damn excited, the smile would not obey my mind and it remained in place. I would look like a grinning idiot, but I gave in to my excitement and decided not to care. My crazy grin almost left my face when I had a moment of panic: what if Jason wasn't there to get me? Oh my God, that would be awful. But, as we slowly came down the jetway, I reasoned with myself that his mother was also involved, so of course he would be there. As I rounded the corner and walked into the receiving gate, there he was! At that moment, he looked like a hero to me. He was smiling and as I got closer, he opened his great big, muscled arms to give me a hug. I ran to him and felt truly happy.

We chatted and laughed and held hands and kissed while we waited for my luggage. He was wearing Calvin Klein's Obsession cologne; it was his signature scent. How ironic, I think now, but at the time, I was there for it. After retrieving my luggage, we headed to the doors that would let us outside, and that's when it hit me. There it was: that woodsy, floral, salty aroma of California. I think it's caused by the Cedar trees, but I could be wrong as there are many fragrant trees and plants to give credit to. Whatever it was, I found comfort in it. I'm guessing the reason has something to do with my childhood memories of being in Southern California with my grandparents.

We drove "home," to my new home, and I insisted on keeping the windows down. I wanted to smell that fragrance as long as I could. It was warm in California, sunny, and there was, of course, no sign of the bleak winter that was around the corner in far, far away Minnesota. In that moment of freeways and sunshine and palm trees and traffic and overpasses and blue bird skies, Minnesota seemed a lifetime ago. We drove inland, and about 45 minutes later, we were turning on to a little street, and there, down the block, was where I would live from then on. We parked in the driveway, and when I stepped out of the car, I realized how hot it was. My nylons and miniskirt and long-sleeved silk shirt were certainly all wrong. I couldn't wait to get inside and change clothes.

Funny, or maybe not so funny, I never considered how Jason's brother would feel about me living in their home. It's truly startling to realize how self-absorbed we are in our teenage years. I think victims of trauma can be especially selfish, as they have learned from the age trauma occurred, that they must come up with a way to self-advocate, do their own acquiring and fulfill their own needs, because no one has done it for them.

So, there I was, feeling excited, important, **special**. Jason brought me in the house and showed me around. It was a rambler, with three bedrooms and two bathrooms. There was the kitchen and dining area, which we saw right away when coming in from the garage. There was a backyard, but it was rather dry looking and ill-kept. I soon learned that California was going through a draught then, (and ever since, I think) and no one was watering their lawns. We put my things in Jason's room, where I would be staying with him. As a parent now, I cringe at how his mom may have felt, but I would meet her later, and she was super nice. Maybe she liked having a girl around because her house was always full of boys.

Jason's brother Andrew was also there; he was friendly, but not overly so. He wasn't rude, he just wasn't sure what to think, so he mainly observed. Andrew was younger than Jason by a year or two, and they looked completely different. Andrew was tall, lanky, and blond, whereas Jason was not quite as tall, and beefy instead of lanky, with dark features. I tried to be friendly, but I felt a little defensive of my presence there, so I became quiet for a while. I didn't want Andrew irritated that I was now living in his home, so I think maybe I tried to draw as little attention to myself as possible.

Once my things were deposited in Jason's bedroom, I changed (now I was wearing a pair of short Guess jean shorts and a tee shirt) and we went back out to the garage. Jason had his weight-lifting equipment in the garage, and I would discover this is where we would mostly be hanging out.

Within the half-hour of being at my new home, the boys from down the block came over to check out Jason's new roommate. Jason introduced me to Brandon and Eric, and right away, I noticed a few things. First, they were twins. Second, they were hot- way cuter than my boyfriend. Third, they were very friendly and full of smiles and welcoming things to say. Jason proceeded to inform me that Brandon and Eric were always over. You mean, I was to spend my days here, with these college boys being at the house often? If the girls from Minnesota could see me now... You see, on the Range, I was Sara

Morgan, the uncool brown girl who didn't have confidence. Here, I could be whomever I wanted. So instead, I was Sara Morgan, with the killer bod and the fiery, flirty personality. They didn't have to know I was a nerd. Brandon and Eric would come over and they would all lift weights together in the garage, listening to Two Short, LL Cool J, Digital Underground, EPMD, Stevie B, and Tony! Toni! Toné! among others.

I met Jason's mom Maryanne that evening when she came home from work. She wore scrubs, and she looked just like Jason, except she was tiny, and had blonde hair. They had the same eyes and the same smile. She was very nice, and basically gave me the shortest speech in the world about expectations. The rules were so few, it felt like I was living with roommates instead of a parental unit. The main thing she was concerned about was telling me not to take long showers because of the draught, and that water was very expensive. I swore to myself I would be the perfect permanent house guest. I didn't want her sorry that she let me live with them.

Jason was in college, and he also worked at the now defunct Orchard Supply Hardware. When I first arrived in California, I didn't have a job right away, I think Jason's mom wanted to let me settle in and get in school first. I learned that Jason paid "rent" to his mom, which I found interesting. I get it now, as he was no longer in High School and was working. Yes, he was in college, but I knew living in California costed way more than living on the Iron Range in Minnesota. Jason's brother Andrew worked at Roundtable Pizza, and to this day, aside from Vi's in Biwabik, Minnesota, Roundtable Pizza is my absolute favorite. There is nothing like it, and it was amazing that we could get pizza for free or super cheap basically any time we wanted.

Alas- soon came the day that I would have to go to school. I think I arrived in California on a Friday and then started school on Monday. I would go to Ygnacio Valley High in Concord, and it was within walking distance of our house. Ygnacio Valley High was a school with approximately 1,500 kids grades 9-12 during 1990. In comparison to many other schools, it's not a lot of students. However, to me, it seemed like a massive amount. I was coming from a school where there were maybe 300 students total in grades 9-12. This was a big change for a small-town girl. I braced myself for the stares, the whispers and being the brown girl.

When I arrived at the school, I noticed so many things all at once. The school buildings were so flat! There were not levels, everything was spread out. The classes were in different buildings and to get from one class to another, you walked out the door into the sunshine and to another class across the way or down the sidewalk. It was very much like a college campus. There was a big quad area where I would later learn that kids would go to eat outside and hang out. The school office was **huge** compared to my little school up north. I had never seen so many secretaries in one place. Once I got my class list, I headed to my first class, which was psychology, I was feeling enthusiastic about that. My heart was pounding with nervousness, and as I pushed the door open, I realized at once that my previous fears were for unfounded.

The classroom was full of kids of all different colors, I was not the brown girl by herself anymore! There were Mexican kids, Indian kids, black kids, white kids, Asian kids, and Italian kids. No one stared at me like I was different! I was shown to a seat and after about a minute of getting my information straight, the teacher proceeded with the lesson. I absorbed everything he said, because I found psychology to be fascinating.

The rest of my classes were similar in that I didn't stick out from anyone else, and the kids were friendly. They even started calling me Brenda, as in Brenda Walsh, a girl who moved from Minnesota to California on a show that just came out called Beverly Hills, 90210. I laughed and just went with it, and many of the kids asked me about Minnesota. I told them about the cold weather and the snow, and I could tell they were intrigued. The only time a few had seen snow was when they went to Heavenly at Lake Tahoe. I was in the middle of a tale of how small the town was where I came from, when suddenly, there was a piercing alarm that rang through the speakers and across the campus. I watched in horror and panic as all the students took shelter under their desks. I sat rooted to my chair as I tried to process what was happening around me. I slowly came back to myself as I heard the teacher tell me to get under my desk.

Was this the end of the world? I squeezed my eyes shut, waiting for a missile to hit. I squinted one eye open when the alarm stopped, and I heard kids laughing and talking and getting back in their seats. I followed suit, no longer the brown girl because I was sure my face was drained of all color.

The teacher saw my confusion and told me not to worry, it was just an earthquake drill. I looked at him like he was an alien. My mouth agape, I finally found my voice and asked in a rather shrill decibel, "***How do you know when you're about to have an earthquake?***" Now it was the other kids' turn to look at me like I was the alien.

"You don't **know** it's going to happen, it just happens," said one of the boys who I later learned was named Dario. I felt a bit stupid, but I held my head high and was determined to never make that mistake again. Cheese and Rice, I still had to get through lunch.

I was a lucky duck. I had had so many credits from going to school in Minnesota, that my class load in California was a piece of cake. I had only 3 serious classes; Psychology, Economics, and American History. The other classes I had alternated days of either weightlifting or dance class. Then I was free to go home an hour early because my day was done.

And so, I got through the school days, in a school where kids cared more about their grades and futures than they cared about their social status. The star football player was also in drama class; the cheerleaders weren't snobby, and no one was made fun of for being smart. Some kids missed school because they were going on auditions for movies or TV. There was fast food offered at lunch. There were celebrations of different cultures set up throughout the year. The school colors were bright yellow and royal blue, and I was now an Ygnacio Valley Warrior.

14

The Girl & the Aria

School out in California was a huge change for me, not only in number of students, but also by way of events they put on. My new school was giving a dance presentation, and I really wanted to go. My boyfriend had to work, so I went alone. I didn't have any friends to go with yet, but I was curious about a presentation like this.

On the night of the dance show, I arrived at the large gymnasium and found it completely transformed. These kids out here were something else. Look, my daughter's high school has around 3,700 students, and I have never seen them put on something like **this**. The whole place looked dreamy- an underwater scene of someplace far away. It didn't look like the "under the sea" corny decor that birthday parties or even prom can have. It was more sophisticated. There were fishing nets, shadows of large sea creatures, and rock formations. There were these lights that gave underwater gentle wave effects against the ceiling and the walls. It was like walking onto an ocean floor. I looked around me in wonder, excited about the performance I was about to see.

All at once, over the speakers, was this burst of music that engulfed the entire space, with voices climbing and soaring to magical places. I was utterly still, goose bumps appearing on my arms despite the warm, early California evening. I had never heard anything like it in all my life. It was exquisite, crystal clear, a bit melancholy but triumphant at the same time. I found that I had tears in my eyes, but I didn't even care, the sound of the soprano voices was so achingly lovely. I didn't understand a word of what they were saying, but I didn't need to. This was a song about hope, love, beauty, and freedom.

For the first time in my 17 years, in the ugly, painful, and deceitful world I was used to, I was given a taste of something that instead was good, magnificent, pure, hopeful. This world was completely void of anything bad. In those four minutes of my life, I was free from my past, from the lies my mind told me about my worth, from anyone who could hurt me. So moved was I, that I found the DJ who was supplying the music for the event and asked him the name of the song.

"Aria," he said somewhat distractedly, seeming slightly annoyed that I was bothering him. Then he looked at my expectant eyes and saw I wasn't leaving his booth. "By Yanni," he finished dutifully.

I had never heard an Aria before, and I smiled knowing I was going to find the CD and buy it for myself. It didn't matter that this made me a nerd, I was used to that. I didn't care that I was probably one of the few 17-year-olds that discovered this kind of music and loved it. All that mattered to me was that momentary relief from the dark places in my mind. I was so moved and excited, and yet when I realized I had no one to share this with, I felt a little bit sad. I was very alone. No one would understand how I felt because I didn't fully understand it myself.

After time, I did start to make a few friends, some of whom I'm still friends with today. School was an entirely different experience than I had been used to, and for once, it didn't suck. I admit, I did skip school on occasion. I would go with Jason and the boys to Santa Cruz for the day and while they played football on the beach, I would sunbathe and listen to the ocean.

I even went to my senior prom. I made my boyfriend take me, because in the movie *Pretty in Pink*, Iona had stressed the importance of going to Prom. So we went, me in a horrible white dress, and him barely dressed up at all. Prom was held at the beautiful St. Francis Hotel in San Francisco, not a gymnasium like back home, and it was truly elegant. I was so thrilled; I had never been anywhere so glamorous before. We sat with a few of my friends, but we didn't stay long. Jason refused to dance, even though there was a DJ and a great light show. With no one to dance with, the point of being at prom was kind of moot. Even more disappointing, was that on the way home, we went through the drive-thru at Jack in the Box. I was very disenchanted, because this was supposed to be a special night, but it sure wasn't. I'm sure it all seemed terribly dull to Jason, being five years older than me, and to him, that mattered more than my desire to experience new things.

I graduated successfully, and that in of itself was a very different experience than it would have been had I been in Mt. Iron, Minnesota. Our graduating class was large, and graduation was held in a big pavilion. My parents flew into Los Angeles and stayed with my grandparents, then they drove up to watch me walk across the floor and accept my diploma. I thought I was cooler than I could even describe, and like an idiot, I wore shades as I walked proudly down to accept my freedom from school. Looking back, I feel pretty cringey about that, but, hey- they were Oakleys, and that had to count for something right?

After graduation, I went and visited my parents and grandparents at the hotel they were staying in. My boyfriend Jason didn't come with me, I can't remember if it was because he knew my parents didn't like him, and it was a mutual decision between himself and me, or if it was because he was a coward. In hindsight, I think it was the latter. Jason was a coward. Sure, he was big and strong and physically intimidating, but when it came to truth and facing the people he'd wronged, he was a coward. You can't solve everything with your fists, and this was one situation he couldn't fix his way. I also seriously doubt my parents had any desire to see him, so maybe it was for the best.

It was awkward sitting there with my parents, feeling like I should visit but knowing I was out here against their wishes. It was not lost on me that I should feel somewhat meek in that I knew my previous behavior had been aminable, but at the time I couldn't reconcile the thought of being respectful to the nth degree with the ability to be so.

I visited with them for what I know was not long enough, most definitely not the length of visit they deserved, what with them being my parents and making that long trek to watch this milestone in my life. I couldn't get out of there fast enough because I was so uncomfortable.

They did give me a graduation present, which stumped me for all time. I think I took it back to the room they were staying in and opened it. I can't remember for sure. In any case, I was surprised with the contents. They gave me luggage, which was truly nice; I wish I had appreciated that more, because good luggage is almost a necessity. (Well, not really, but it sure is nice to own.) They also gave me a pen— a **pen**. I didn't know what to think about this. I'm an over-thinker, and this one sent me. Should I be insulted? Should I take it as they wanted to hear from me in letter form? Did they want to give me a gift that wasn't something I could use, to prove a point? Were they trying to tell me how little my life mattered to them now? No, that couldn't be, they had come all the way here to watch me graduate. Were they trying to give me something that would equal my importance? What would a 17-year-old do with a pen, albeit a nice pen? I still don't know the reason for that pen, and I avoid asking these things now that I'm older because the past is not always fun for me to think about- or bring up with the people I hurt with my actions. Therapy is helping me with this, but it's a slow process.

So, after my parents left and headed back to LA, (I admit I was relieved) I sheepishly retreated to the house I was calling home, with my boyfriend and the boys from around the block. We went and got pizza that night, and a few bottles of booze. There would be no sad evening for me, the Minnesota girl, living a life of sunshine and warmth and ocean breezes. As we drove down the busy streets of Concord, I gazed out the window, letting the night caress me in its lights and sultry, velvety air. *If only everyone back home could see me now*! I smiled to myself. *What a life*, I thought, *what a life!* My trauma was far, far away, tucked in a little neck of the woods in Minnesota, and for the most part, it finally left me alone. I was truly happy for a while.

The Girl, Funny Guy, & the Surfer

This is the part of the story I'm not thrilled about writing. Some of it is funny, although horrible, and some of it truly lets you in on the type of person I had become due to lack of boundaries, lack of supervision, and being emotionally stunted whether by my choice or not.

Eventually, after graduation, Jason and I moved into a condo that belonged to his mother's significant other. We were glad to be on our own and living by ourselves, and I'm sure Jason's mother was not bummed about the fact that we were out from under her responsibility. I was working at the Sunvalley mall, at a little store called The Accessory Place. Jason was still working at Orchard Supply Hardware, and we somehow made ends meet.

As time went on, I started to outgrow the relationship with Jason, and he started hanging on tighter than ever. There were incidents that happened that I'm not going to get into, simply because I don't want to get sued, being as he is alive and well and still residing out west. What I will say is that ***my*** recollection of these things that happened were violent, physically painful, and emotionally frightening. One of the boys from around the block, Brandon, came and rescued me when I needed it the most, and to this very day, he has a piece of my heart for doing that. I don't know what would have become of me if he hadn't stepped in and helped me. I don't like thinking about it.

Oh, I wasn't an angel while living with Jason, I'll admit to that. In fact, I was probably one of the shadiest girlfriends to ever roam the earth. Did I deserve what was coming to me? No, I absolutely did not. What I will take responsibility for, is that I should have swallowed my pride and called my parents and gotten out of there. I don't know if I didn't do that entirely because of my pride, or my inability to go back to a place that represented sexual abuse at every turn. For whatever reason, I stayed in place and decided the best thing to do was to cheat on Jason. The bastard deserved it, I thought. Maybe he did, but I can say today that I shouldn't have been that unkind to myself. But the story is a funny one...

Ok so I had gone out with a friend from my work. Her name was Lisa Sullivan. She looked exactly like Malibu Barbie. She was tall, blonde, gorgeous, and she had big blue eyes with a little pert nose and heart shaped lips. She was 10 years older than me, but we hit it off famously. She could get me into the bars as well, so when Jason was at work, I would go out with her, (before things got very volatile between me and him, and I couldn't do anything at all.) Anyway, on one outing, I met this guy at the bar she got me into. He was decidedly older than me, but he was an absolute riot. We were laughing all night long. I do not know **how** we decided to go out on a date, how we managed it. I didn't tell him about Jason, and no one had cell phones at the time, so he must have had my phone number, the house one I shared with Jason. I wince thinking about that.

So, there I was, getting ready for my date with funny guy. I can't even remember his name. As luck would have it, I decided to wear my fuchsia silk shirt and my little spandex black skirt, black nylons, and cheap black heels. Yes, the same fuchsia silk shirt my dear grandma wore and fell into a pool in. I should have left that stupid thing back in Minnesota.

Jason and I lived in our condo in a gated area. The gate opened with a code or a remote, and it opened right onto Clayton Road, with room for one car in the length of space from the road to the gate. Also, there was a stop light immediately to the right once you exited, or, if you were coming down the street, the stop light would have been right on the corner the complex existed on. I couldn't very well have funny guy drive into the condo to get me, I didn't have the remote, I didn't want to give him the code, and I didn't want anyone seeing me. I asked him what kind of car he drove, and he told me it was a red mustang with purple lights around the license plate. He said he would be down at the front at 7 p.m. Ok, I thought, this is cool, I'm going out with an older guy in his mustang!

7 p.m. neared, and I had made my way down to the entrance of our condo complex. I saw with chagrin that it was chilly and cloudy, and I didn't have a jacket. *Too late now*, I thought, as I went outside my gate and looked for his car. Now Clayton Road is three lanes across going in one direction, and three lanes across going in the other, so it was quite a busy street.

I didn't have to wait long, because there it was, early even, the red mustang with purple around the license plate. I was annoyed he was in the middle lane. *What an idiot*, I thought, *I'm going to have to run out to the middle?* The light turned red as he approached. I was thankful for that; it would make my stupid path to the middle lane easier. I clutched my black purse and ran across the first lane, yanked open the passenger door, and climbed in. As I grabbed the seatbelt and looked over with a smile, the lights turned green, and traffic started. My smile froze on my face as I realized this was **not** funny guy! This was someone else, an even older dude with curly dark hair, a porn 'stache and a look of sheer terror on his face!

Now I don't know who was more scared, porn 'stache guy or me. He clutched the steering wheel so tightly that his knuckles were turning white, and his ass had risen off the seat, he was clenching his butt cheeks so hard. I noticed at this time that my hand was deep inside my purse, I don't know why that was, and I'm guessing he thought I was getting out a gun or some such weapon.

"Uh," he stammered, "where are we goin'?" I felt like a complete fucking loser at this point, I was **so** annoyed at myself, and annoyed at him. What are the chances there were **two** red mustangs out there with purple around the license plate? It was bad enough there was one! Why did this guy have to own one as well? This was **his** fault, I reasoned.

"You can drop me off at the next lights," I snapped and stared straight ahead. The next lights were coming up quick, it was only one big block from where he picked me up. This had all happened within seconds. He quickly maneuvered over to the right lane, and to both of our relief, (probably more his judging by the terrified look on his face,) like clockwork, the light turned red, and I hopped out, mumbling "thanks" as I stepped onto the sidewalk. I took no more than two steps, when the sky opened, and it started to pour on my perfect hair, my perfect makeup, and my cursed fuchsia silk shirt that had seen it all. *Great*, I thought, *just fucking great*. I walked my way back on what now seemed like a long block in my black heels with no jacket, and just as I reached the lights in front of the entrance to our condo, there it was—the red mustang with purple around the license plate. He was in the far-right lane, and if I hadn't been so visible, I would have just ditched the guy and gone upstairs where I could lick my wounds in peace. However, now that he had seen me, and I'd seen him, and he knows I've seen him, I'm committed to the situation.

I opened the passenger door, hopped in, and gave him a little smile. He looked a bit shocked at my appearance, and then he said, "Where **were** you?"

"Oh, I just needed something from the store, so I walked up there and grabbed it," I lied, my tone too bright. I acted like I took walks in the rain every day of my life.

The jerk side-eyed me and goes, "I could have driven you there."

I put on my best pull-me-up-by-my-bootstraps look and said, "Oh it's no problem at all! See? Time saved." I managed to fluff my hair a bit, and nonchalantly asked him to run his heater on high so I could dry my shirt.

Needless-to-say, that was our first and last date. Funny guy did not find me so funny.

Another time I decided it would be beneficial to go away for a short weekend with a guy I met at my new job at the Danville Hotel Restaurant. His name was Mike, and he was a surfer. This was my first and only foray into the surfing world. Point Break had just come out and I congratulated myself on riding that wave at the height of its popularity. (See what I did there?)

Mike was cool, he had dark hair he kept in a man bun (before they were a thing) and he had piercing eyes the color of aqua. He looked like a model for Billabong, and I was unsure how I gained his interest. I could not pass it up, no matter what situation I was in, and as far as Jason knew, I was off with a friend. What a total asshole I was, my God! Jason was a bit suspicious, but hadn't yet descended into his worst self, so I had a bit of freedom still.

Mike picked me up super early on a Saturday in his Saab (of course he drove a Saab) and I, a little over-dressed, jumped in, bag in tow. We were going to the beach for an overnight. I envisioned him surfing the ocean waves, with me on the beach, lounging on a blanket with a picnic basket full of delicious romantic food. We would laugh and play and maybe he would pick me up and carry me down to the water, where we would end up on the sand, like in the movie *From Here to Eternity*.

As it turned out, that was not to be the case, at **all**. We arrived at the beach, where we knocked on the door of a little apartment. It was answered by an unkept guy in his late 20's. He mumbled something that sounded like "come in," grabbed a backpack, and said he wouldn't be back for a few days. Mike threw his things on the bed in the living room, and I followed suit. I looked around the tiny space for a picnic basket or something that would suffice, but saw nothing but empties here and there, a Kool-Aid pitcher on the counter and a loaf of bread beside it. The place smelled musty, and sweet, like incense and something else I couldn't identify. The couch had sunk in toward the middle, and I immediately wondered if I had made a mistake.

Mike opened the fridge and grabbed a bottled water. He offered me one, and I took it silently, still unsure of how to feel. He was all grins, in his happy place clearly, and started to strip down. I hated that as annoyed as I was, I couldn't help but notice his jawline and the way his dark hair fell over his face. Mike had a beautiful nose; I notice noses because I had always wished mine were smaller. He turned his back to me, dropped trou, and proceeded to pull on some swim shorts. It was practically the ass-crack of dawn, and he was already going in the water? He then pulled on a wet suit and started talking to me about how great the waves were going to be because it was chilly and windy. I smiled and nodded, wondering what I should be doing. I had wanted time with Mike, the bed looked inviting, unattractive as it was with its brown bedspread, but it would seem my daydreams of a leisurely morning basking in the afterglow would not happen.

Mike was finally all zipped up, and with a grin and a contented shrug of his shoulders, he motioned toward the shelf. "There are books if you want to read, you can watch whatever you want, Kai has cable. Take a nap if you like! Oh, and there's a few things in the fridge if you get hungry. Mostly peanut butter but we can eat when I get back later too!" He quickly grabbed a piece of bread and a very ripe banana and wolfed them down. I sat there, open mouthed, realizing that Mike was headed toward the beach, and I was going to be stuck in this dank apartment with a couple of New Age books, old records, and a little TV. But not to worry, Kai had cable! I was not happy. But, in the interest of how beautiful Mike was, and not wanting to make him regret choosing to bring me, (at the same time regretting my choosing to come) I smiled brightly and told him to enjoy the day. "Come out if you like! Bring a blanket because it's cold," he said, as he headed out the door. I watched through the window as he unstrapped his surfboard from the roof of the car and started walking down the sandy trail toward the ocean.

That was the most boring day of my life. I watched a little of Kai's cable, but I couldn't concentrate. I pulled down a few books from the shelves, but none of them interested me. I did take a long nap, and mercifully time slipped by. When I woke, I used the bathroom, thankful Mike wasn't there to know I was a human who pooped. I took a shower and reapplied my makeup. I made half a peanut butter sandwich and watched a little more TV. I finally decided to head down to the beach. Slipping on my sandals and grabbing a blanket, I made my way in the direction I saw Mike go.

After a long and sluggish journey through shifting sand, I could see the heads and bodies of surfers bobbing in the waves. I wrapped the blanket around my shoulders and sat crisscross on the sand. It wasn't Point Break, but I did love the sounds of the ocean and even the seagulls that cried out to each other. The waves were quite nice, even a non-surfing girl could see that, and I could understand why Mike hadn't come back yet. Finally, when the wind died down and the waters remained calm longer between swells, I saw him. He emerged from the water like a God, and with his surfboard tucked under his arm, he made his way to me, smiling from ear to ear. It was then that I knew this was it for him, nothing could come close to this as far as he was concerned. Any girl by his side would have to be content to wait her turn.

Mike and I ended up going back up to the apartment, where he showered and changed. I was so turned on by his surfing and the way his wet dark hair fell around his face, I could hardly stand it. I was glad when he mentioned going out to eat, because I needed something to satisfy me. At dinner, I pretended to be all shy and pure, asking innocently, "I see there is only one bed… where will we both sleep?" He looked up at me and smiled, and then he gently brushed a few hairs out of my eyes. I could feel myself melting.

"Awww," he said softly, "you're not a bimbo… cool." I sat there a bit stunned. I had hoped he would come back with something flirty and suggestive, but no, he was pleased that I was worried about sleeping together. This was not what I had planned at all.

Once we were back at the apartment, I watched incredulously as he made up a sleeping place for himself on the couch, intending to give me the actual bed. We did cuddle on the couch and watch TV, and as we kissed, I turned up the heat as much as I could. He sat back, looking in my eyes and asked, "Are you sure?" I said I had never been surer of anything in my life. Silently, I had never been surer of the fact that my afternoon was dull as rocks. I had never been surer that I was ignored all day. I had never been surer that if I were to be his girlfriend, I would come second to the ocean. I had never been surer of the fact that I needed kissing and everything else.

    The next day, he drove me home in mostly silence. It wasn't bad, it was just quiet— final. He smiled warmly as he dropped me off, and as I got out of his car, he told me, "Don't be a stranger!" I knew that was the last I would see of Mike. He didn't even come back to work. I also knew then that I **was,** in fact a bimbo, uncool.

The Girl, NWA, Mary Jane & the Cop

After some more cheating on my part and behavior on his part that was quite terrifying, I was finally able to make the move out of our condo, away from Jason. It was a scary time, physically and emotionally, as he seemed to be obsessed with me. It took some clever doing, and some help, but I did it. They say that leaving a volatile situation is the most dangerous time, but I survived it, like everything else I had survived.

Like I said, I was working at The Accessory Place in the Sunvalley mall with my Malibu Barbie friend Lisa. She knew I was in a bad spot as far as my home life, so she helped arrange for me to stay with another girl who was working opposite shifts of me. Her name was Stephanie, and she lived across the street from the mall in a house with her mom, her mom's boyfriend, her sister, her brother, and her little boy. I was shocked they would even take me in, but they must have been told about my situation being a bit of an emergency. I barely knew Stephanie, but we would soon become fast friends. I packed my suitcase and we arrived at her house via Stephanie's Oldsmobile. It was a boat, it was old, and we loved it because it represented freedom. Later, we would cruise around in that car we lovingly referred to as "the Automobile," all because we would crank up NWA and sing "My Automobile" at the top of our lungs as we would gad about the city.

I would sleep on their couch, and as the days turned into weeks, our friendship grew. I watched her son for her when she was at work or had some place to be. He was just a little guy, brown-skinned with a shock of dark hair. She would call him by his full name in such a loving tone, that I couldn't help but fall in love with him as well. He had a big grin and seemed to be smiling all the time. His dad would pick him up on the weekends, which meant Stephanie and I had time to do whatever we wanted then.

I won't say much about where I lived, but I will say that I tried to help as much as I could. I would clean and take care of things to the best of my ability. I never wanted to be a burden. What little pay I would earn I had good intentions of giving to Stephanie's mother. I did give her a bit, but I had to eat as well, and then there was the Mary Jane and Mickey's beer. I had to have money for **that**! My 18-year-old brain had good intentions, but poor delivery when it came to paying more rent. I rarely ate there, in fact, I rarely ate. Mostly we partied, and it was not long after that I first tried weed.

We were at a party, which was nothing new as there were parties all over the place and Stephanie seemed to know everyone. Anyway, we were at a party, and someone whipped out a pot pipe. They passed it around and I was panicking as it came my way. I wasn't panicking because it was a drug, I was panicking because I didn't know how to smoke it. I watched as it made its way from person to person, not knowing what I would do when it landed in my hands. I had already had a few Mickeys, (don't ask why I drank Mickeys because I have no idea) but I had not caught a buzz big enough to mask my apprehension. In no time, it found its way to me, along with a lighter. I looked down at it, looked up at a few of the faces at the table, and finally said in a voice filled with embarrassment, "I don't know what to do."

Stephanie looked at me through glassy eyes and grinned a bit too big. I could see she wanted to laugh, but she spared me and instead said, "Awww… a newbie! That's so cute!" She then proceeded to come over to me, giggling, and showed me the way. Absolutely I coughed, of course I did, and everyone had a good chuckle at my expense. *Oh well*, I thought, *everyone was a newbie at one time*, and my turn was almost over. As the night went on, I kept waiting to feel whatever it was I was supposed to feel, but I never did. Thankfully I had my Mickeys, so I was able to catch a buzz and party like a rock star.

It was that night that I met Scott. He had curly blond hair and blue eyes; he reminded me of Ian Ziering from Beverly Hills 90210. I was smitten. He was laid back and cool, very goofy and best friends with the guy Stephanie was into. In no time, we were a fun foursome, hanging out all the time and going to parties. As it turned out, Scott was a free spirit, and I couldn't tame him. After only weeks, our budding romance permanently drooped and died, and after a few tears, I was on to the next guy. There were guys all over the place, and I met a few interesting ones.

The second time I tried smoking, I was absolutely **baked**, and in no time at all, I became a pro. I used to enjoy it immensely, and

Stephanie and I smoked every weekend she didn't have her son. We would hang out with different people, often looking over the city or laying in a big park looking up at the stars. I have never been one of those cool, chill people when I smoke. Nope, I'm one of the people who erupts into gales of laughter, to the point where my voice is squeaky, and I have tears running down my face. I hated it, because sometimes I think I would harsh someone's mellow. Mostly they laughed with me, but every now and then someone would tell me they couldn't handle me, and they would leave the room. Sometimes I stumbled across a particular strand of weed that would help me chill and softly laugh at appropriate times, but that was rare. Aside from my inane giggling, I recall one other time I annoyed the crap out of people. It was the first time I tried a water bong, and I blew **into** it instead of sucking **out** of it. No one was pleased.

As time went on, I made more friends outside of Stephanie, which was good because sometimes she had places to go, and I wasn't invited. One night, I went into the city with my new friend Tina and her cousin. In San Francisco, there are plenty of clubs you can get into that are 18+, and I was ready. After a night of strobe lights, loud hip-hop and eye candy, we decided to head back while there was still time to find something to do closer to home. Tina had driven us there, and when we left the club entrance and walked down the noisy streets of San Fran, we realized that something was very wrong. Her car wasn't where we had left it. After a bit of time changing direction and heading down other streets, we had to admit the obvious: her car had been stolen. This was so not ideal, so not cool.

We ended up going to the nearest cop shop and the cops assisted in helping us fill out the necessary paperwork. One of the cops, whose name was Mickey, (like my beer of choice, weird) was quite flirtatious and asked me for my number. *Why not*, I thought, I had never dated a cop before, and this could be interesting. Plus, he was cute and had a contagious smile. When I think about him, I think about the lighting in the cop shop that night. They were fluorescents, and the walls were painted a shade of seafoam, and instead of being irritating, it was somehow… appealing. Isn't that strange how we remember things that seem to be of no significance, but they stand out in our minds and connect us to a moment in time.

Mickey was nice and drove us home, all the way back to Concord. After that, I didn't go out with Tina again, but I did go out with Mickey. About a week later, he again came to Concord from the city to get me, which still surprises me. It's easily a half-hour drive, and when you live in California, that seems long. I chuckle now thinking he must have really liked what he saw. Anyway, he brought me back to the city, and I was thrilled, because this was such a new experience for me: dating a cop. What would we do? I'm not sure what I envisioned, but the night ahead wasn't it.

We went to a neighborhood of the city that was decidedly… "rough." I had to keep reminding myself that Mickey was a cop, and I was safe. He took me out to dinner at some place I would appreciate now as an adult, but as a hopeful 18-year-old on a date with a man who had an actual career, I was unsure what to think. The restaurant was a total dive. It was even in a garage type of setting; literally the front was a big rolling garage door that opened to a small area with plain cement flooring. There were bongos playing from somewhere and a little kitchen in the back that was open for all to see before that type of kitchen became a desired aesthetic. Pretty sure in this case, they couldn't be bothered to put walls around it or couldn't afford to do so. The walls were painted blue, and there were pictures hung here and there. The clientele looked like they wandered in off the streets, and I felt very over-dressed. Little did I realize as a young me, that this would surely mean amazing food.

It occurred to me that maybe this was what Mickey could afford, so I tried to just enjoy myself and stop being so expectant. The food was extraordinarily delicious, and most definitely Hispanic. From which country, I couldn't tell you, but it was for sure from somewhere in South America. Maybe I didn't get my candle-lit dinner, but this place served great food, so I started thinking I was lucky to go there.

After dinner, Mickey asked me if I wanted to go and listen to some live music- of course I did! I couldn't imagine where we were going, as he was not giving me any hints. I ran through all kinds of concerts that might be going on, and the more I thought, the more excited I became, as I thought maybe he had tickets to someone really cool and didn't tell me. Maybe we would see The Red Hot Chili Peppers, or R.E.M. or even LL Cool J! For a girl living paycheck to paycheck, staying with a kind friend, and not even owning a vehicle, I sure had lofty expectations. As it turned out, he took me to a little warehouse on an unassuming street. With my breath stuck in my throat, we went in a shadowy side entrance and down some wooden stairs to an old, heavy door. Mickey paid an entrance fee for us, and we walked into a dark, enormous room. There were spotlights and strobe lights in the corners, smoke from a fog machine in the air, a not-so-permanent looking bar in the back of the room, and folding chairs in rows toward the front. The music was loud, and the band on stage was rocking in the style of Jesus Jones.

I was speechless, which was good because if I had anything to say, I would have had to shout, as the music was so loud. I saw so many different people with eclectic fashion choices, and from what seemed like all walks of life.

Mickey grabbed us some seats and then shouted to me, "Do you want a drink?" I could have used a drink, but I told him I would have a Coke. He smiled and said, "Do you want a **real** drink?" I shook my head no, as my mind immediately went into gumshoe mode- worried he was trying to trap me. He knew I was 18, and I wasn't about to let him make a citizen's arrest. Would it be a citizen's arrest- since he was off duty? I laugh now thinking about my suspicious mind. Perhaps the **wiser** thought was to maybe not have any kind of drink at all, because, A., who knew what could be put in it, and B., don't get drunk with someone you don't know. But instead, I was being Sherlock Holmes from Britt Minnesota, worried about being arrested at an underground makeshift bar.

Mickey returned with his drink and my Coke, and I sipped on it as I watched him really getting into the music, even pumping his fist in the air. I tried getting in the mood as well, but there was just too much strangeness going on around me for me to let go. As I stood there, in my preppy, fun outfit that was all wrong for this place, I was stunned to see Mickey reach in his pocket and take out a tiny container. He proceeded to open the container and remove a joint. I watched in absolute shock as he pulled out a lighter and lit up, grinning out of the corner of his mouth as he glanced over at my startled expression. He took a few quick puffs and offered it to me. Again, I declined, worrying about smoking pot with a cop.

"You sure? It's good stuff!" He grinned, looking in admiration at his doobie.

I shook my head no, and said, "I'm trying to cut back."

"Right on," he nodded and took another puff.

We stayed for a long while at this place, longer than I wanted to that's for sure. Afterwards, he drove me home at my request because I was feeling so weirded out by dating a cop that offered an 18-year-old booze and drugs. As he dropped me off, he kissed me and then said, "I have a question for you, and you can say no…" I took a deep breath and smiled, *what now*, I wondered. Encouraged, he said, "Do you mind giving me a keepsake?" I know I looked confused.

"A keepsake?" I asked, wondering that the hell he was talking about.

"Yeah," he said softly, a smile in his voice. "Can I have your bra to remember you by?" He slowly traced the outline of the strap that was showing on my bare shoulder; my top had slid off to the side *Flashdance* style. Being as the entire night was kind of a shit-show, I thought, w*hy not? I don't even care at this point.* If he really wanted my bra, fine. I reached under my shirt, unclasped the back, pulled it off from underneath and handed it over. It was one of my favorites, sea-foam green like the walls in the cop shop, with ivory lace on the overlay. He grinned as he held it. I shook my head with a half-smile on my face, opened the passenger door, and ran up the sidewalk to safety of the house and my friend Stephanie who was probably waiting to hear all about my date.

Today as I write this, I wonder where that bra is. I imagine he's told everyone that he had a crazy night of sex with an 18-year-old. Maybe it hung on his wall for some time, maybe he tucked it away in a drawer with a bunch of other bras from other girls. Maybe he wears it, who knows. At this point in my life, anything was possible.

17

The Girl, the Rave, & Vibrating Guy

At Stephanie's house, her mom was becoming more and more irritable. Looking back, I'm sure she had a few things to be irritated about. I knew her and her boyfriend were fighting more, so she seemed to be more stressed than ever. I suspected she was planning on leaving him. In addition to that stressor for her, I wasn't paying enough rent, and when I did pay, the check bounced, and I panicked. Somehow, I had managed a snowball effect with my checking account at Wells Fargo. One thing bounced, causing an overdraft that caused another thing to bounce, which caused another over-draft and so on. I'm not gonna sugar coat it, I was playing beat the bank, and it didn't work in my favor. I wasn't working enough hours, and I didn't have enough money to pay rent and have anything left over at all, for anything. I was eating as little as I could, and I would go out on dates to get food here and there. I wasn't being responsible; my brain functionality was stunted. This happens with trauma victims, oftentimes, their maturity will stop at the place where they were traumatized the most, or where they could no longer move forward until past trauma was dealt with. I'm no therapist, but I would guess I was stuck somewhere around 14 to 16 years of age.

By this time, I had been fired from The Accessory Place. **That** happened because one day, when I went into the store for my opening shift, I neglected to open the garage cage in the stupid step-by-step process that needed to happen. First, you had to unlock the sides, then you had to depress a button on the side that would start an automated electric lifting of the cage. I forgot to unlock the sides, and instead just depressed the button. The gate started to lift but ran into the locks. It only could lift by about 3 feet before it jammed. This caused the store to have to call in a maintenance person, who didn't arrive until a few hours later. The mall imposes a fine on stores that do not open at the regular hours, and I think the store got hit with a fine or a very stiff warning. Not only that, but I had cost the store a few hours of revenue. I was no longer an asset, I was a liability— goodbye, me. This is about the time when the checks bounced. Thankfully, that very day, I managed to land a job at JC Penney, also in the mall.

Stephanie and her family hadn't moved out of the house quite yet, they were mid-planning, and so I still had a place to stay. One of my last outings with Stephanie involved my very first rave. We went with some friends up in the mountains, dressed to party. I had just received my first paycheck from Penney's, and I had a bit of cash.

I had never seen anything like what we experienced that night. We arrived in the dark wooded mountains, with high, cliff-like rocks on all sides among tall trees and sensual warm air. There was a DJ playing a remix of "Twilight Zone" by 2 Unlimited, and the spots and strobe lights were nothing short of epic. The lights shot through the tall trees, making their leaves look like they were dancing. Everyone had glow sticks, and many people wore very tall hats like Dr. Seuss characters. There was a light show being played against the side of a cliff, and people danced everywhere. There was smoke in the air from a fog machine, and I thought there was never a cooler place to be in all my life. There were people walking around with lollipops and candy baby pacifiers. I wouldn't know why until later in the night.

Stephanie, myself, and our friends danced and drank, I don't know who drove us there. I had to work the next day, but I didn't care. We ran into someone selling the drug ecstasy, and like a **complete** idiot, I bought one hit. Even my friends were surprised at my wildness. None of us knew that life had made sure I was aware that I had no value, so I didn't value my precious life.

I had never done ecstasy, or "E" as they called it, and I wanted to forget my troubles of where I would live, not having a lot of money, and not much to eat. I wanted to just be free, and to have a break from the constant anxiety I felt. So, I bought "E" from a total stranger, and took it by myself. No one else in my group did. I kind of felt like a badass for being so daring. About 40 minutes later, I was "rolling." (That is the term for riding the high ecstasy provides.) I am not going to go into details, because there's no way I want to glorify drug usage. I'll just say that for a few hours, there was nothing bad in the world. I had a massive dopamine dump to the brain, which I found out later was not a fun come down at all. When your brain depletes its dopamine levels, there is no more "feel good" chemical left, and that leaves you feeling sad, weepy, tired, and super depressed. After I started rolling, it was then that I was clued-in to the use of lollipops and candy pacifiers, or even soft, non-edible rubbery ones. You're feeling so much energy from every ounce of your being, that to not pull stupid faces or bite the insides of your mouth, a lollipop can help relieve that urge to jaw clench.

Side note: on the rare occasion, doing ecstasy or MDMA can kill you- even one dose. If you don't die, you could be rendered a total vegetable, for life. I didn't know this at the time, and I'm so thankful God was looking out for me, even then, because here I am. Back to the story...

Eventually, the cops broke up the rave, and we went home. That morning, I went to work, feeling like complete and utter shit. My skin felt like it was greasy. My hair felt limp. I could feel everything on my body all at once. I was hyper aware of my scent, and worried that others could smell me as well. It wasn't a bad smell; it was just different. (Or maybe the smell **was** bad, and my nose wasn't working, I don't know.) The roots of my hair felt alive like I had used tea tree shampoo, and I couldn't get enough fluids. I would drink so much water, but it seemed like I was a dry sponge. I felt like none of it was being absorbed. I looked terrible, I had bags under my eyes and a bit of paranoia had set in because I hadn't slept yet. Thankfully, my shift ended, and I was mercifully able to go home and lay down. I slept through the night until the next day. It took a few days before I felt like myself.

By the time I was back to normal, Stephanie's mom and her boyfriend finally broke up, and that meant that moving out plans were now in high gear. They would be moving out of Concord, to Pleasant Hill. Her mom's new boyfriend said I could stay for a few weeks, but then I would need to move out. I would have nowhere to go. I felt shame and embarrassment, even hurt. The other problem was that if I lived in Pleasant Hill, I could not get to my job. It was so convenient living across from the mall and being able to walk to work. The mom's former boyfriend didn't mind if I stayed **there**, but it would feel awkward and it felt disloyal to stay with "the enemy." By default, I was bound to my friend and her mother, even if I **was** a moocher.

I was hurting, and back then, I didn't know where this hurt was coming from, no one owed me anything. I understand now that I felt rejected, unwanted, and abandoned by the new rule that although I could stay for a few weeks, I didn't belong. I wasn't part of anything, I was being "given up," much like I had been at the beginning of my life. I was seeking solace in the arms of anyone who was able to give me comfort, even if for a night.

One evening, I went on a date with a customer I met at work, his name was Andrew. Andrew was 28, ten years older than me. He picked me up in his BMW, and we went to dinner and then back to his place. To this day, I can't believe no one trafficked me, I hung out with so many people I didn't know. Andrew played U2 on his stereo and asked me what I thought the lyrics to *"Trying to Throw Your Arms Around the World"* meant. I had no idea, nor did I really care. I later found out Andrew had a thing for spanking and being spanked, and I didn't feel like this was going to fit into my agenda. So, after he tried to unsuccessfully persuade me to go out with him one more time, I took my leave, and swore off older guys for a hot minute.

That minute turned out to be the shortest minute known to man.

I met another guy through Lisa, at a bar I had no business being in. He was beautiful, he was a fun time; the kind of guy that would lead the entire bar in an impromptu conga line. He ended up asking me out, and I agreed, even though he was much older than me, in his early 30's maybe. He kept referring to me as "just a baby," which holds such a creep factor that I can't even think about it now without grimacing. Yet, he was a blast, and so there I was, being picked up for a date with him. I don't even remember what we did, but I do remember ending up back at his place at the end of the night. I can't believe that despite all of times I went places with strange guys, I never was beaten or harmed. It was only the ones I knew that seemed to do that to me- odd.

Anyway, we were at his place and things were getting decidedly hot and heavy. We were in his room, and the clothes were hitting the floor. As he was kissing me, and about to make **the** move, I unexpectedly heard what sounded like croaking from outside. Was it a **frog**? Then suddenly, I heard and more accurately **felt** something vibrating, loudly. It was coming from his lower back, and it along with the croaking, startled me so much, that I yelped and shot up like rocket. It kept making a loud "zzzzzzz" sound, and in the darkness of the room, I went into full flight mode, bounding out of the bed and running in circles trying to locate my clothes. Because I had startled him as well, he only added to the terror and confusion by loudly shouting, "**What?? WHAT??** He probably thought we were being attacked from some unseen enemy. His yelling only made me scream again as I desperately looked for my clothes.

I somehow managed to find my skirt, which I probably pulled on both inside out and backwards, my cheap, black high heeled shoes, and my white button up shirt, which I threw over my body. My bra dangling from my fingertips, and my shoes in my other hand, I managed to leap over the bed and slide the window open. The screen was no match for my panic. I pushed it out of the window and leapt down to the ground, landing in the grass, barefoot. Now I was in full hysterics as I remembered the croaking noise. Were there frogs out here? I broke into a sprint for the cement sidewalk.

"**HEY!!**" He yelled out of his window, "***Don't you want me to call you a cab?***" Even amidst my bizarre outburst, he was ever the gentleman.

"*I'm good!*" I shouted back, running into the night.

I do not know how I made it home that evening. I really can't remember. I just know I was completely traumatized by whatever had just happened. I have no idea where that buzzing and vibrating came from. I think it was a device on his back to help with back pain maybe, I don't know for sure. It may seem silly to you, and in fact, it's a funny story; but this is how my brain worked during that time. If I wasn't careful, trauma would rear its ugly head and catch me unawares.

The Girl Goes to Vegas

Ok, don't ask me how I swung this, but I ended up going to Vegas with Malibu Barbie. Tickets to Vegas were cheap from San Francisco, anywhere from $50 to $75. I believe I was supposed to pay her back later when I could. I was game to go because Lisa was so much fun. She was such a guy magnet, and I knew it would be epic. Her mother and her aunt were going as well, and we were able to stay in a room with them. This was super generous on Lisa's part, because I was in such a bad place in my life and had no one. Stephanie and I were growing apart, mainly because her mom was angry about me not meeting my rent obligations. I'm sure when I took off to Vegas it put her right over the edge. I'm so sorry to her mom, like- genuinely so sorry.

We arrived in Vegas and stayed at the Excalibur. It's a little off the strip, but we didn't care. We went down to the main floor, where there was dancing and a bar that had a show. There was booze everywhere of course. So. Much. Free. Booze. As it was, there was an Air Force base close by, and the place was loaded with pilots. Lisa and I had a blast, we were girls about town, and no matter where we were, we were dressed to kill. We did venture out of the casino to see Hoover Dam, which was enormous and treacherous looking, but the fun times were on the strip. By the second night, I was ready to run away with an Air Force guy that I had just met. He was going to Germany and asked me to go with. I know now that he wasn't serious, but at the time, I had nothing to lose. In addition, I had no passport, so I didn't know how I thought I was going to do that. I was so ignorant.

When we came back from Vegas, Stephanie's mom could hardly look at me. I managed to be scarce, working as much as I could at JC Penney's. I knew that very soon, I wouldn't have a place nearby to stay at, so I had to give work my notice. On my second to last day at JC Penney's, I met a nice guy who came in looking for a belt. I'll call him "Brad," because his real name is just as "white sounding." He was tall, dark, and good-looking, and he had a gentle way about him. He took me out, and for the first time in a long, long while, I felt like he really saw me, **me**, the lost girl. He seemed to know I was hungry, both for food and for someone to love me. He was in the army and stationed at the base not far from Concord. Brad and I spent the weekend together. He was Mexican, but oddly, his name could not be further from his culture. We listened to a lot of C&C Music Factory, and ate at Denny's, where we would share a plate called Moons Over My Hammy. We would sit on the waterfront of Monterey Bay and just visit. Back then, we were innocent in the ways of love, with neither of us having any real experience with an actual grown-up relationship. I had been through life, and he had been a soldier, and the start of us seemed like there were no flaws at all. I felt like maybe I would keep this one.

Back home, once again, after Stephanie's family loaded up the moving truck, Malibu Barbie came to my rescue. Lisa told me I could stay with her, as I had nowhere to go. She was in the middle of a move herself, to Crockett, California. Crockett was about 25 minutes from Concord, and only had a population of about 3,500 people. It is famous for C&H Sugar, and that's about it. I really liked Lisa, and since I had no other real options, I gratefully went and stayed with her. I packed up my suitcases from my parents, (the ones they gave me at graduation) got in her car, and we drove to Crockett. She was staying with her boyfriend, a well-to-do construction worker with a beautiful, big house he was in the middle of remodeling. He was gone most of the day, and I believe Lisa was as well. I was jobless and was in possession of my very last paycheck from work. I didn't know what I planned on doing. Where would I find a job, and without a car, how would I get there if I did?

As the days went on, my dwelling situation became… tense. Lisa was not getting enough sleep, and I hadn't yet been able to pay her back for Vegas. I figured it was only a matter of time, my days at her house were decidedly numbered. I won't say too much about that house, except to say that there were some not-so-great things happening, and when Brad came to stay a day or two with me there, he told me I needed to call my parents, and go home. He was the first person in all of California that wasn't selfish. He cared enough about me, to say what needed to be said: "go home." It was exactly what I needed to hear, that's all it took. I remember I called my parents and asked to come home, and the next thing I knew, I had a ticket back to Minnesota. I don't know how I got to the airport. I just knew I was going home.

The Aftermath

At this point in the story, I am having feelings. The next part of this book is painful to write, as much or even more than the first part. That said, I am going to start off by saying this:

Don't fucking judge people when you don't know the burdens they carry. My complete lack of appropriateness when it came to relationships, responsibility, and grown-up things, was a result of being absolutely stunted by the trauma in my life and receiving no help for it. I didn't know how to seek out help without having to talk about the things that had traumatized me, and I could not talk about the things that happened to me. Instead, I chose a life of running, partying, and escaping the possibility of having to face things and look them in the eye. My life choices were partly due to a tender, sheltered upbringing and being ill-prepared for the bad things in life. No, this isn't me blaming my parents per se, I am telling you that they did the best they could with the tools given them from their parents and environment and so on.

When you have been raped, molested, harmed, physically abused, and emotionally abused, it is difficult to be a grown-up. It is difficult, if not impossible, to raise children. It is difficult to pay bills on time because you are escaping life. It's hard to remember to do the things that need to be done, as you are used to blocking out moments in time, big chunks of life… even writing these memoirs is an extremely difficult task for me. I must dig, dig, DIG into the recesses of my brain to remember time frames, what came first, what events happened in what order, what I want to share with people and what I cannot. It is difficult to write without seeming defiant, defensive, and protective of myself. There have been many days that, after hours of writing, I fall into bed, my emotions and my mind completely drained.

You may even ask yourself, "Why is she doing this? Why is she sharing these private things?" Because damn it! Because these things need to be talked about. As a society, we do not address abuse, mental health or the fall-out from abuse enough. Without therapy, this is what can happen to people who are dealing with too much. We need to keep creating safe spaces for people to talk, get help, and heal. If my story can encourage even one person to get help when they need it, or maybe encourage another to give understanding and compassion when someone else needs it, then I have succeeded.

So, keep these things in mind as I limp through Part Two of this book.

19

The Girl Gets to Eat

Once I had my plane ticket home, I had to say goodbye to Brad. He was kind and good, and truthfully, I can't remember if we made plans to keep in touch or reconnect at another time. I just knew I was going home. I was thankful for the fact that he had taken care of me that last weekend I was in California. He had fed me, gave me shelter, and pointed me in the right direction, as I was so very, very lost.

My flight home was a red-eye. I had a layover in Vegas, and by the time I de-planed at Las Vegas airport and found my gate, I was exhausted. My eyes were scratchy and irritated, and as I looked around me in the wee hours of the morning, I could hear the bells and whistles of the slots being played in the all-night bar close by. I smiled dryly, and for a moment I remembered the sounds of Vegas when I was there with Lisa, the slot machines and laughter and cries of excitement. I thought of Air Force guy and rolled my eyes at the stupidity of me thinking I was going to Germany with him. Shaking my head at myself, I spread my sweatshirt down on two chairs, and laid on my side on top of it. I looped my arm through my carry-on bag and vowed to just "rest my eyes." I was hungry, but of course had no money for food. My stomach growled in protest, but I steeled myself against it. *I would eat when I got home*, I thought.

After what seemed like mere seconds, I felt someone gently shake my shoulder. I looked up and saw a kind-looking man's face above me.

"Is this your flight? It's boarding," he said, glancing up at the gate. I was wide awake then, and, looking over my shoulder, I saw that the empty gate was now full of people who were lined up like sheep boarding the plane. I sat up quickly and turned to thank the man that woke me, but he was nowhere. I looked in all directions, but there was no sign of him. I felt weird, like I had imagined it all, but something told me it had really happened. I had such a feeling of oddness, and as I write this, I wonder if it was my imagination, a dream, an angel, or a super-fast running guy. In any case, I didn't have time to ponder.

Once boarded, I looked out my window seat into the darkness of the sky. I wondered what would await me at home. I had no idea how I would feel. Would my parents be mad at me, and if so, how long would that last? Would they support me while I looked for work? How would I tell them I had no money? That would be humiliating. Mercifully, I dozed off again, in spite all my worries.

The screech of the tires on the runway woke me, and the knots in my stomach from my nerves made me feel like I would vomit. I forced myself to get it together, and I exited the plane with the rest of the weary travelers. I got my bag and saw that my brother had been sent to pick me up. I was mildly annoyed. I'm not sure why they sent him and didn't come themselves. I thought of many reasons. One, maybe because I had come home during the week, my dad had to work. Two, maybe my parents were **that** mad, that they didn't even want to see me right away. Three, maybe I wasn't worth them coming themselves. Fourth, maybe they were worried they would get there, and I wouldn't have taken my flight. I wasn't thrilled that it was Aaron that came to get me, but what could I do about that? We still had a four-hour drive home, and I just knew it would be awkward. I deserve this, I thought, as I tried holding my head high.

We made a stop at Tobies, which is a restaurant/gas station that is the half-way point between the Twin Cities and the Iron Range. Aaron brought me to the restaurant part, and I was practically drooling, I was so hungry. I know I must have looked awful, wolfing down my big breakfast. I could have eaten another plate, but I was so glad to have finally eaten something, I didn't ask for more. Thankfully Aaron paid; I wasn't sure if mom and dad told him to, or if I said I didn't have any money. Either way, I was so hungry, I didn't care about my pride right then.

We drove in silence the rest of the way home, and as we went, I rolled the window down. This trip home was like my trip out to California, except in the exact opposite way. I was at once aware of the scent of pine that filled my nostrils. I had gone on vacations with my parents, I had gone to LA every summer and spent weeks and weeks there; I had been so many places, and I didn't know until this moment that Minnesota had a scent. I guess I had to have lived somewhere else for years in order to appreciate the wonderful, clear air of Minnesota, and the way it was like looking at the world through glasses that had just been cleaned. For the first time in a long, long while, I associated something positive with Minnesota. Alas, it would take decades longer for the feeling to come back. I didn't know that then, and I closed my eyes and drank it in. I must have closed my eyes for more than an hour because I woke to the car coming to a stop in the driveway of my childhood home.

At once, I felt my nerves come alive with fear and apprehension. *Here we go*, I thought. As I went down the steps of the driveway toward the front door, I held my breath. I walked in and discovered that no one was there at first. I set my things down, and as I did so, my mom came down the steps. I looked up at her through eyes that I'm sure had bags underneath them, and I tried to read her face. She neither looked upset or happy, just reserved.

"You look terrible," she said, broom in hand. I was taken aback, and at once was aware of my thin frame, my unwashed hair, the lack of color in my skin, and my large eyes. Not eating regularly had taken a toll on my appearance, I was now sure of it. Still, I was hurt by her observation, and felt like a complete and utter failure. I was right about my dad being at work, and it was probably better that he was.

Once in my room, I laid down on my bed, in the familiar surroundings of home. It was so quiet. There were no freeway sounds, no busy streets, no honking, no shouting, no loud music, no jets flying overhead, only the rustling of the trees and the occasional muffled voice of my mother downstairs, probably talking to my dad on the phone. I got up and looked out of my window seat. There was the dark blue lake, happily bouncing along with the breeze, making lapping noises at the dock. The ocean that I had come to get used to felt like light years away.

It may have been in another lifetime as far as my brain was concerned.

Again, I laid back down in my bed, and curled my legs up underneath me. Memories came flooding in my mind. I thought about my ex-boyfriend Jason, and his mother. I wondered what he was doing and if he knew I left California. I thought about the boys from around the block, especially Brandon, and I wondered if they knew that all I wasn't cut out for the life I had so valiantly set out to live years ago. I thought about the many escapades I had and was so glad that no one here knew "my number," as in the number of guys I messed around with. With sadness, I realized that I wasn't even sure if I did. I thought about Lisa, and hoped she would find happiness. The last I had seen her, she was angry at me, and was looking for something in the house that she was unable to locate, slamming drawers and doors as she frantically searched. I thought about Stephanie, her little boy, and her family who had taken me in. I wondered if they were going about their day, giving no thought to the Minnesota girl who they had gotten to know. The sites, smells, and feel of California haunted me, and in my childhood room in Minnesota, I felt very, very alone.

While living in California, at the beginning, I didn't watch what I ate. I ate like a normal teenager I suppose- sporadically. As time went on, I started to watch what I ate so that I could be perfectly thin in the right places. As more time went on, I didn't eat much because I had very little money and was on my own. I started to like my pin-thin figure. I even started to take to it like a mother to a child. I watched in wonder as my wrists became as small as a child's and my waist was as tiny as a pre-pubescent girl's. I welcomed the ache and burn that came with hunger, mainly because I felt like I was in control of it. I could determine whether my body would obey me. I decided if I would feel full, or feel hunger pains, and when they obediently happened, I felt like I was once again the captain of my own ship.

    I don't know how much I slept the first weeks I was home, but it was an exorbitant amount. All I did was sleep and eat and drink orange juice. I started to put on some healthy and much needed weight. I couldn't get enough meat, and my parents probably thought I would eat them out of house and home. I did not have an immediate plan for my future, I wasn't sure what I was going to do. The first few weeks were a bit awkward for me and my parents, but I could tell they were trying to know me as I was at this point in my life. I was also trying but found that I barely had anything in common with them. I had become a different person, and they seemed like strangers to me. I was sure they wouldn't want to hear about my adventures in California, and I didn't really want to talk about it with them. I most definitely didn't want to talk about the things that happened before I moved to California, so that left very little to discuss.

    One day, I borrowed their car (this time with their permission) and went to town. I needed a couple things, and I suppose my parents gave me some money to get them, as I did not have a job yet. I went to the mall, and as I walked around, I felt its smallness. There was hardly a soul there, it was very quiet, not like the bright and busy malls I was now used to. I was kind of glad for this because what I really needed to buy was a pregnancy test. Sure enough, my stupid period was either late or not going to make an appearance at all. *Stupid, stupid me*, I thought, as I bought my test and went into the mall bathroom to take it. I watched in sickening anticipation as first one line appeared on the stick, and then, a dreaded second line showed up. I sat still and bit my lip, taking it all in. *Welp, this made sense,* I reasoned. No wonder I was constantly sleeping, constantly hungry, and a bit off. I felt better knowing **why**, but now I had a whole new dilemma. How would I tell my parents?

The first thing I did was call Brad in California, to let him know that he was the lucky guy that got to father my child. He took it surprisingly well, and even seemed happy about it. That made me feel a little bit relieved. He assured me that he would tell my parents, and then, with a smile in his voice, he said, "Well, I suppose we should get married." The idea surprised me because I hadn't gotten that far in my thinking. Knowing my parents, however, this was what they would expect from me. You don't get pregnant without being married, and, since I liked Brad enough, even felt like I even loved him, I agreed.

True to his word, he called my parents on the phone, and told them they were going to be grandparents. The shocking thing to me was that my parents took it even better than Brad did. They knew about Brad, I had told them earlier that he was the reason I called them to ask if I could come home, so they already appreciated him for that alone. Now that he gave them the news of a grandchild on the way, they seemed happy for me, for them, for us. Maybe in their minds this was a good thing because I would be taken care of, I would settle down, and they wouldn't have to worry about me, I don't know.

Brad's plan was to get out of the Army when he was able, and then to drive to Minnesota. His parents were living in Illinois at the time, and they would drive up for the wedding. It would be a small affair, in my parent's downstairs porch. Until then, I would live with my parents, and they would take care of me. Thankfully, I was able to get on Minnesota State insurance, and they covered pre-existing conditions like pregnancy. Now I could go to the doctor every month and monitor the progress of my pregnancy.

Brad arrived in Minnesota either late August or very early September, because we were married on September 5, 1992. The morning of our wedding, I remember going upstairs, and my dad was in my parent's bedroom.

"You know, you don't have to do this. We will take care of you," he said gently. To this day, I wonder why he said that, because it went directly against what I thought they would expect from me. In that moment, why I didn't take him up on that offer can only be explained by guilt and the desire to finally do something right. I needed to be honorable and not bring any more shame to my parent's good name.

That winter of being pregnant, I enjoyed eating food regularly and without fear for the first time in years. All I wanted was meat and potatoes, real "feel good" foods. When hunger hit me, it would be like a vicious attack, like nothing I had ever experienced before. I watched as my belly grew with the life inside of me, and when I felt the baby's first kick, I was over-joyed. We knew we were having a boy, and Brad couldn't be prouder. This is a Mexican thing, having a boy is considered the best thing to happen to a young married couple. Brad's dad kept half-joking, half-seriously telling me I better be "making" a boy in there, and with annoyance, I informed him that science says whether I had a boy was up to the dad, as he determines the sex of the baby. That bought me silence from him on the matter for the rest of my pregnancy. He didn't need to worry though, because Anthony was born on April 10, 1993. I was 19, and terrified.

20

The Girl is a Mom

Being a young mom was something I was not prepared for. I took to it, though, and found a new kind of love that I didn't know existed. I didn't know how I was going to be responsible for such a little guy, it was very overwhelming to me. I was newly married, and newly a mother. I was all the things that made me uncomfortable. I felt a kind of young love for my husband though, and for a while, we were happy together. We visited his family with our baby, their first grandson. We even went on a trip with them to Yellowstone National Park. My dad gave Brad a job at his company, and he learned how to install siding and windows. We lived in a little apartment on the main street of Eveleth, close to my dad's business. Eventually, we bought a house, and in no time, we were expecting our second child.

Chloe arrived in May 1996, and with her, came the sun. She was a good baby, an easy child, and we were very happy. For a bit of time, I played the role of the happy housewife and even enjoyed it. We had become friends with another couple, and we would do dinners at each other's houses. Everything seemed like it was not so bad, but then entered a few moments that caused trust issues. For me, being a victim of abuse, I had a hard time dealing when things were not completely transparent. I hated being lied to; even little white lies would send me over the edge. Poor Brad's fate was that he would never measure up to what I needed, as I didn't even know what I needed exactly. I just knew I needed something, and he wasn't cutting the proverbial mustard.

Brad was not an angel by any means, and I blame him for 50% of our failure. However, I held him to damn near impossible standards, and when he failed to meet them, I lost it. These things led to dissension in our daily interactions. Soon, I found the idea of being tied to the family lifestyle "challenging" at best, "repulsive" at worst. I had barely matured at all from the teenage girl I was when I left for California. I still wanted to be free to do what I wanted to do. That wasn't always an option when you had a husband and two little children clinging to your side.

Because of our trust issues, and neither Brad nor myself being mature enough to handle the marriage; along came an incident that there was no coming back from. I found myself visiting my parent's house, alone, to let them know the inevitable. I was going to file for divorce, too much had happened, and I couldn't, or wouldn't fix it. My parents took the news as I figured they would. They told me I needed to stay and work it out. They couldn't imagine why I felt that was not an option. They were not happy at all, and no matter what I told them, they were quite upset. I didn't expect them to support my choice, but I did hope they would support **me**, their daughter.

I won't go into details of the deeper problems of this marriage, as it involves someone else who isn't given a place here to speak. I can only tell you my story, my experience, and where I was coming from. Had we both been more mature and less selfish, perhaps we could have made the marriage work, repaired the damage. and learned from it; yet there we were, two kids in their twenties, refusing or unable to grow up. I would be the first person in the Morgan home to get divorced, and I'm sure the shame that brought that upon our family name was not fun for anyone to bear. I remember telling my grandma, and for me, that was the scariest of all. I can't remember what she said, but I somehow survived it.

If I thought marriage was tough, I was unprepared for being a single mom. I was very attached to my kids, as during our marriage, Brad worked for my dad, and I stayed home spending my time with our children. Now I had to work, which meant I would be away from Anthony and Chloe for the first time on a regular basis. I had also become a bit of a "pariah" in many church people's eyes. Previously, I had been a black sheep and a rebellious teenager, but my return from California, my "happy looking" marriage that lasted a few years, and my beautiful children had all raised my social score. For a time, I was welcomed among the flock of sheep at my church. This divorce, however, shot me right down to a level that made it so now people looked at me cautiously. They backed off, invites for dinner stopped and people didn't bother to make small talk with me when I would show up at church. I started not going to church as often, and when I did go, I would arrive late and leave early.

By this time, I had found a new job that I was very much underqualified for, and a new boyfriend who I had no business being with.

The new job was Monday through Friday, 8-5. It was in Aurora, and I lived in Eveleth. This meant a little drive for me every day. I was to be a secretary/front desk person, and I was to know Microsoft Word, Excel, basic bookkeeping, and the ability to keep on top of ordering office supplies. I was 24 years old. While my friends were off at college, and possibly already graduating with their degrees, I had been home changing diapers, wiping mouths, and cooking dinners. I knew nothing about anything outside of that, and although I interview well, I had no idea what I was doing.

Because the job was 8-5 every day, I would have to put the kids in daycare. That was more than I could stand. In the end, they would stay with my parents during the week, and I would go visit them after work. This was a lot of driving for me. In the morning, I would be driving to Aurora for work, back home, and then to my parent's house, and then back home for a total of around 88 miles. I wouldn't always go out to my parent's every day after work; it was too much driving for my shitty car and too much gas money. Plus, I felt guilty when I would go. I can't speak for my parents, but the impression I got was that they were just extremely disappointed in me. My mom was never good at hiding her facial expressions, I don't think she even tried. She always looked annoyed at me and frustrated that I was living this life. No one was more frustrated than me, I can fucking assure you.

I also felt guilty because I liked that this arrangement gave me an opportunity to live my life, without the responsibility of child-care every day, but with the badge of goodness that I felt motherhood carried. I was supposed to get my children every weekend, but as time went on, I was not always doing that either. Oh, I would go stay with my mom and dad for a while and visit with the kids and spend time with them, but I wouldn't always bring them home. I was just overwhelmed with where my life had taken me, and it was difficult to be around my parents, feeling the shame that I felt.

Fortunately, or unfortunately, I was fired from my job. I had resorted to almost begging them not to fire me, and when that failed, I asked if I could at least stay out the day. The answer was no. I was not performing up to par, and they let me go. There went my income, as child support was not always to be counted upon. Brad was having his own struggles, and I think being divorced by me, living in Northern Minnesota where he had no family, and being given the job of every other weekend dad did not agree with him. I'm not making excuses for him, but he was young and immature as well, and I can't say with certainty that he was just a complete loser in totality. The things we do as young people, even sometimes as adults, can only be judged by one person, and that isn't me. Karma is also a player in the game, as is the law, so... I guess when our time comes to pay the price for our decisions, it will happen. In the meantime, I just knew that I needed to get a job.

I had taken in a few roommates as well. One was my friend Jeanna, and one was my boyfriend, Chad. Up until me losing my job, we had all managed to get by somehow. We lived in the house I had bought with my ex-husband, and it seemed to be ok, until I lost my job. After that, it was one big, fucking mess. I **still** had no sense of how to live life successfully. I **wanted** to; I just didn't know how. I couldn't cope with responsibility, the muchness of it. Furthermore, there was another thing that happened. I was pregnant, again. I was on birth control, but not everything is guaranteed.

I don't know why we ended up having to move out of the house. I think I was behind on house payments, and the bank was not happy about it. Brad had agreed to talk to the bank, catch up the house, and move back in. I would move out with Chad. Poor Jeanna, I don't know what she ended up doing, but I felt horrible about it.

Chad and I found an apartment on the Northside of Virginia. It was a duplex, and we had the upstairs. I found another job, at the Virginia Clinic, as a switchboard operator. My job would entail me taking calls and routing them to the right people or sending messages up to the nurses for them to return the call. There were two very nice ladies who helped train me in, and while I worked, Chad would watch the kids for me. I think he worked in advertising, and he could set his own hours. It wasn't glamorous; I knew he was making up hours and not really doing a great job. What I didn't know, is that he wasn't being all that good to my kids. He basically just had a short fuse, and his own issues, and didn't give them love or show any real interest in them. I think their days with him were lonely, even scary, and I'm sure they felt lost.

In time, at the advice of my manager, I was strongly encouraged to quit my job at the clinic. This came after I took a message for someone who called in, wanting the doctor to call her back. I could hardly understand her.

"I need to speak to the doctor about my igjawwieee," she

mumbled.

"Excuse me," I said, "can you repeat that?"

This upset the lady even more and she practically yelled at me, "I SAID I NEED TO SPEAK TO THE DOCTOR ABOUT MY AIRPEEECE!!"

I typed the message to the best of my ability and sent it on up the chain. When it arrived on the fourth floor, and the nurses got their hands on it, I'm sure there was rolling of the eyes and laughter all around. My note said: "So and so needs to speak with the doctor about her hair piece," and I put the patient's name and number after it. As it turns out, **NO ONE** needed to talk to the doctor about their hair piece. **Herpes-** yes. Hair piece, no. It wasn't my only failure, and they pulled me aside for the talk. I would need to get it together ASAP, or maybe find another line of work.

As my pregnancy grew, my relationship failed. Pretty soon, Chad couldn't be counted on. I never knew if he was coming home, or even where he was. I could never get a hold of him. I had to quit my job at the clinic, I couldn't afford daycare, and I had no one to watch my children. I was on state assistance, but it wasn't enough. There were times when I would send my kids to my mom and dad's- if only so they could eat. There was never enough food, and I was washing clothes in the bathtub with bar soap. I was broke, alone, pregnant, and ashamed of where I was in life. I watched as my friends went on trips abroad, as they got together and seemed to lead their happy lives. I didn't feel sorry for myself really, I just felt left behind, forgotten, and not good enough. They were pristine, I was dirty and tainted.

One day, my dad came to visit with me at my apartment. I was just informed that I would be evicted. I had known it was going to happen. I couldn't make rent. Chad was basically gone, and there wasn't any way I could count on him for help, even though I was carrying his child. My dad walked up the stairs to my place, and as he emerged through the door, I felt a heaviness I couldn't explain. Maybe it was intuition because I knew this was a different kind of visit.

He seemed sad, awkward, and defeated, or maybe he was mirroring me. What happened next is taken from a blog I wrote, and I share a bit with you below.

(Sarita Vargas, I Once Held You in My Arms, November 18, 2021, www.saritasiren.com/myadoptionjourney)

"After what seemed like hours, he finally he managed to ask me what my plan was for after I had my baby. I had no plan.

I... had...no... plan.

I do not remember the exact words of our conversation, but the gist of it was this: My dad said that a couple that was a friend of theirs, (and known to me) was wanting to adopt another child. They already had one child they adopted and wanted that child to have a sibling. I had known this couple from my childhood. They were maybe 10 years older than me. They were on a waiting list, I believe, and my dad hinted that perhaps this could be an option for my situation.

   Wait. I need to say a few things first. Firstly, I was going to regular checkups at the clinic with this pregnancy. I was watching and feeling this baby growing inside me and although I was barely with his father any longer, I loved this little being in my belly more than I knew I could. Secondly, my parents love their grandchildren, my other two children. They would love this child just as much. This wasn't a situation of "this baby wouldn't matter like my previous ones did." This was a situation where my parents lovingly looked at the reality of my circumstances, and based on the dismal display of living I was doing, they were probably worried for this baby. Ok that's what I needed to say. Back to the story.

At first, I was shocked and felt like I had been slapped. I felt angry, hurt, sad, relieved, worried, upset, sick. I think my dad took my kids with him that night… or was he dropping them off… I cannot remember. I just remember feeling gob smacked. I hated him in that instant, hated him for even suggesting this. My heart hurt, and my pride was taking a fiery dart like it was being hurled with all the force of an accomplished warrior. The reality of my life was more real that day than any other. The blow to my ego, my pride, my ability to be a success made my psyche come crashing down all around me. This story is painful to tell, because I blocked a lot of my feelings out of those days. I could call and ask my dad and mom what I said or did, they probably remember even if I don't. I can't do that though because it still pains me. I don't want to know.

I just remember eventually agreeing to do this, because I felt I would never be able to give this baby anything good. It did not seem fair, no matter which angle I looked at it from. Anthony and Chloe were so little, and having divorced their father only a bit before, they were dealing with their own things; they did not need to deal with mine. I said nothing to them about it. This unborn baby did not need to be brought into my chaotic, unsettled world. Yes, I knew the baby was a boy, and I had been super happy about that. I also knew that housing him would be impossible if I didn't figure things out right away. I was at the mercy of people who held no great fondness of me (my current children's father, and the father of *this* baby). The chances of a pleasant transition to another home weren't looking promising.

I remember telling my OBGYN - Dr. Passal, about my choice. Dr. Passal was very special to me. He never judged me, not once. He never made me feel as if I were "less than" because of this pregnancy. He admired my choice; he let me know that I was doing a brave thing. I needed to hear that because I certainly didn't feel brave. I felt like a giant failure.

Oh wow, this story is incredibly humbling to write! I'm normally a very private person about my past, my life, my choices, and my traumas. Yet, this story needs to be told. For all who are adopted, and all who choose adoption, this story needs to be told.

There were people with clipboards and notebooks and forms and files who got involved once the decision was made. I had to sign so many things, so many papers. I only asked that this would be an "open" adoption. I wanted updates and photos every couple of months. I wanted to be able to see him grow up, even if it had to be from afar. The couple he was going to was very kind. I do not believe I could have made this decision if he were going to complete strangers. I knew they would love him and never abuse him, take care of him, and give him everything I could not. That was my only comfort. I knew they would teach him about God, and I knew he would be given a chance at a good life.

The day came for the birth of my son. The father chose not to be present, and instead, a dear friend of mine came with. Up until a few years ago, I had blocked out so much of this event, that I had forgotten she was with me at the hospital! She kindly reminded me that she was there, and since then, memories are coming back to me. She knew I was alone; she knew I needed someone. I did not want my parents there in the room. It was too much of a private moment for me and I had no idea how I would react or behave. It was easier with her there for whatever reason.

Prior to the birth, Dr. Passal asked me my thoughts on holding my baby right after he was born. I originally decided against that; I was afraid I would be incapable of giving him back if I did. Dr. Passal encouraged me to hold him, because studies have shown that women who do not hold their babies prior to them being placed into adoption will sometimes have nightmares regarding the baby. I did not want nightmares on top of the stress and the trauma of it all, so I agreed, even though I was terrified.

I was induced, that was the plan from the start. This way I would be assured that Dr. Passal would deliver him. He had been with me from the very beginning, and I trusted no one else to be a part of this. Also, inducing made it possible for the soon to be parents of my baby to be at the hospital exactly when they would want to be. Not in the delivery room, of course, but there- waiting like vultures in the hallway,

I was sure. That was my attitude at the time, it couldn't be helped. I took no pleasure in feeling that way, but I suppose that is natural.

I had had my two earlier children naturally, without any drugs of any kind. I chose to get an epidural with this baby, because I could not bear the physical pain on top of the emotional pain. Thankfully, the anesthesiologist was there with this big ol 'needle like a superhero, and with a sigh of relief, the contraction pain subsided, and I was able to get to the pushing stage without feeling much of anything. He was an easy delivery, and when he cried for the first time, I felt two huge tears slide down my face. I turned my head to the wall and felt four more fall freely down my face and into the pillow. It felt like everyone had disappeared, and it was just me and that wall. Never had my life felt so void of any color as it did in that moment.

They brought him to me once he was cleaned up a bit and his vitals were taken. He was wrapped in a blanket, and he had a hat on his perfect little head. I looked down at him, and knew at once that he was mine, he was beautiful, and he was perfect. Holding him seemed like forever and only seconds all at once. I tried to memorize every inch of him, I tried to lock his scent away in my mind so that I could think of it later. I gazed at him until they came and gently took him from me, and I don't remember anything after that.

The next thing I remember was hearing the cries of the newborn babies down the hall, and I asked to please be moved to another floor, it was too much for me to listen to. Thankfully they were able to get the ok on that, and I was promptly moved to another room. My baby's new parents came and saw me, I knew they were going to. It was so difficult at the time to do this. I did not want to see them. I wanted to hate them, but I could not. I wanted to scream at them, but I did not. I wanted them to hurt as much as I did, but at the same time, it was so awful that I would not wish that on anyone, especially them. They were kind, sincere, thankful, joyous, sensitive to my feelings, and cautious. I'm sure I told them what they wanted to hear; I don't really remember all that well. I think I may have been a bit curt with the dad, perhaps projecting my own feelings about men onto him. I feel sorry about that now.

Afterward, I went home, alone. It was quiet. It was too quiet. I still had a bit of a belly, and I hurt physically. I felt numb emotionally. It didn't feel real, had it even happened? The court date that followed assured me that it did. Aside from that, I had a pounding headache for days because when they gave me that epidural, my blood refused to clot. That caused a hole that was leaking spinal fluid. That gave me a headache that made me feel like someone was hitting me in the head with a sledgehammer. So, I went to the hospital again, where they administered a "patch" to help seal that hole up. Then I had court. My head had not stopped hurting yet, and when the judge asked me about my decision, he first asked me if I was physically able to even make decisions, because I was wincing in pain. I assured him that I was fine, and to just get on with it. Well, I didn't say *that* to the judge, but something along those lines."

Sure enough, it was official, the father of my baby and I split. It was a relief, and by that time I was back in my house in Eveleth. Anthony and Chloe's dad had kindly agreed to move out of it so that I could move back into it. When I look back at Brad in those earlier days, it is not without regret at my failings in our marriage. Back then, had I felt like there was help and hope, perhaps I could have been better and done better. I think we both were open to change and could have possibly salvaged what was wrecked. But, my pride, and his pride, my need for therapy to heal what had happened in my early life and my inability to cope with having to go to therapy stood in the way of any chance of reconciliation. Also, Brad was dealing with things, and although I cannot and will not try and speak to those things, he was nowhere near ready to be a responsible father and husband to me either.

Now before you go thinking I'm pining away for my ex, I would like to assure you, I am not. I'm only sad for the kids we were, and the stupid things we both did and said to each other. I used to be angry about it, but now, I just wish we had had help and support that we could connect with. Sometimes, although well-meaning, telling two young married kids to "look to the Lord," gets lost in the reality of things. For Christians, that may be a true piece of advice, but it's also important to be reminded that Jesus meets us where we are, and that first and foremost, we are loved and understood. Human behavior is normal, and should be understood and empathized with, not judged and tsk tsked away. Anyway...

Anthony and Chloe were none-the-wiser about the baby and the adoption. I hid my grief and sadness. They were so little; they didn't really have a clue as to what I was up to outside of the things they could see and feel. Life went on as normal, and I was again trying to balance the stress of raising these two children, meeting my financial obligations, and coping with the giant loss of my baby.

Brad and I had a period of good co-parenting. We would visit with each other as friends, and I met his new girlfriend and even became friends with her. When they broke up, he would go on to date not one, but two of my own friends. That was a bit jarring for me, and although I wasn't necessarily **mad** about it, I was annoyed. I felt forgotten, I felt discarded, and I felt betrayed a bit. He had been mine, and while it didn't bother me when he dated girls I didn't know, I did have feelings about him dating girls I did. These feelings weren't enough to cause me to be an asshole or rude to them, but I didn't mind when they broke up either.

The Girl, the New Job, & An "Oops"

Being a mother during this time was exceedingly difficult. I was so very lost, reeling from the loss of my baby, and the judgement I passed on to myself. Anthony and Chloe bore the brunt of my inability to be a very good parent. Oh, I loved them fiercely, and I enjoyed my time with them. I would grow frustrated with their needs, though, because I couldn't even meet my own. How on earth was I supposed to meet their emotional needs when I was an emotional wreck myself? My M.O. was to run, run away from bad situations, escaping the things I didn't want to face. They learned to fend for themselves in areas they shouldn't have needed to. When I look back at the things I allowed, the moments I put myself first, I cringe and I need to remind myself that I'm forgiven, and that although I cannot change the past, I can do good going forward. If I'm not in a good head space, it can turn into a monster of a battle for me, even now.

I was struggling to make ends meet and was often-times not eating again so that there was enough food for the kids. At one point, I was so desperate for help, that I called my brother and asked if he could loan me $50 bucks. His answer was a definitive "no." I was so embarrassed to have had to ask him in the first place, as he and I never talked aside from the occasional forced moments we shared when I would go to my parent's house. If having to ask him was not embarrassing enough, his answer is what drove home the point that I didn't really have a brother. No, not because he wouldn't help me in this instance, but because over the years, he had never expressed any concern or interest in me whatsoever. I do not know why it was this way, as I cannot speak for him. I attributed this to his witnessing my tumultuous teenage years and maybe not understanding or knowing about my abuse. Maybe it was because I was adopted, because before my teenage years, he didn't care to talk to me or acknowledge my presence in any way either, unless he had to. In any case, this was the blow to my being that would take years to come back from.

In order to pay our bills, I landed a job at a bar on the main street of Virginia. The girl who interviewed me was 8 years younger than me, and she was a pit bull. Her name was Kimmy, and she couldn't have been more than 5'2" and 100 pounds soaking wet; she scared the shit out of me. The Sports Palace was looking for a bartender, and although I knew nothing about bartending, I needed the job. I had just lost a huge amount of weight, with the help of The Firm workout series, and a nice little diet pill called Metabolife. I was about 26, and although I had had three children, you couldn't tell because I was so small, maybe even smaller than I was when I came home from California. Ever since I had had my children, I had been on the heavy side, and no one had given me the time of day. That was about to change.

Kimmy hired me in between our interview and her getting up to receive a liquor order. The Sports Palace was the hottest spot to come and hang out back then, and it had an Italian restaurant in the basement. I was so thankful to be offered this job, and Kimmy said to report to work the following weekend. I was told I could wear whatever, and so I quickly took in what Kimmy was wearing. Even though it was summer, she was in jeans and an oversized sweatshirt that she seemed to disappear in because she was so tiny. I was in awe that she seemed so boss-like, despite her size. I had lied to her and told her I knew how to make basic drinks, and as I write this, I smile because later she would tell me, "You didn't even know how to mix a beer." At first, she was right. I didn't even know how to properly fill a glass from the taps or change out a keg. Yet, regardless of my lack of experience behind a bar, I looked forward to the weekend.

I didn't realize how beautiful I had become, until I reported to work that Friday. I'm not saying this to brag, I'm saying it because up until then, I rarely considered myself beautiful. I was the brown girl. My hair was too dark, my nose was too big, my butt stuck out, and I had big eyebrows. Somehow, I had grown into my features, learned how to apply makeup and shape my brows, curled my shiny dark hair, and bought a great push-up bra. My extreme working out had shaped my legs and arms into beautiful, sinewy extensions of myself. My butt was now a **good** focal point, it was shapely, and my waist was non-existent. I had become physically everything society said I should be, but mentally, I still was stunted and had so much to learn.

My first night of work, I showed up in short jean shorts, a sleeveless, multi-colored tight shirt, and a gold thong. I knew that every time I bent slightly or knelt to grab beer from the cooler, you would be able to see the top of my gold strappy underwear. That was important. I was here to make money because I desperately needed it. I was a survivor. I had made it for a few years in California, and I knew how to get what I needed for the most part. The bar would be no different.

Soon, the bar was filling up with patrons, many of them dudes. I flirted my way through that first shift, engaging them in conversation and looking at them through flashing, wickedly naughty eyes. It worked like a charm, and although I was stuck downstairs in the sports bar and not upstairs where the club was, I managed to keep the clientele in place for a long time.

On the afternoon of my first shift, there was one guy that came in who seemed kind and respectful. Sure, I could tell he was interested in me, but he wasn't obnoxiously obvious about it. His name was Jackson, and right away I was drawn to him, because he wasn't like the others, the gross and disgusting others. The others were pigs. I was getting hit on right and left; many of men didn't even try and hide their intentions. They were crude, crass, and said things that the version of me **today** would never tolerate. Many of these men were married, or at least had girlfriends. This part pissed me off like nothing else. You see, I had developed an aversion to hypocrisy. No one was what they presented to the world, no one. I learned through my early years that people are the worst. They go to church, then they molest you. They are the big football hero, and then they rape you. They act like your friend, but they always want to take from you, usually in the form of sex. These men were no different.

Sure, I was a liar, I flirted and gave them quite a show while I worked. I decided that I would start using **them**, there was no way another man would take advantage of **me**. So, there I was, teasing and making promises with the way I moved and danced to the loud music playing in the bar, and it allowed me to bring in enough by way of tips that it supported me financially just working the weekends only.

As I got better at making drinks, and faster with my delivery, I was moved upstairs to the club. That's where I wanted to be, because after a certain time of the night, that's where everyone in town went. I would come in to work, look at the schedule, and see my name on the list for Twisters, which was the name of the upstairs dance club. Usually, it was me and Kimmy working the club, as we were the fastest at making drinks. The faster you moved, the more people you could serve, the more people you could serve, the more money the bar made, and the more money the bar made, the more tips we had in our jar.

This was all fine and dandy at first. I was able to be home with my children all week long. Sometimes we would spend the day at the beach. Other days, we would go to the park. We watched Blue's Clues and Little Bear in the mornings and made cookies and soup in the afternoons. I was still working out like a fiend, and I started shopping for bar clothes in the girls' section. I was a junior's size 0 or a little girl's size 13. For someone my shape and body make up, that didn't look the healthiest. Metabolife was keeping me energetic, and it made my appetite all but obsolete.

Growing up, I told you that I was very much a fan of my grandparents, on my dad's side. I loved my grandparents on my mom's side as well, but since they lived in California, I spent more time with the ones here in Minnesota. I was especially fond of my grandpa. My **grandma**, however, scared the living shit out of me. I loved her, she was a great cook, a wonderful grandma, and a lovely woman. She always smelled so nice, and I never saw her look a mess. She wore slacks or house dresses and always had her hair done in curls. She wore makeup every time I saw her, and she wore nylons. Grandma got away with speaking her mind- and speak her mind she did! Grandpa was always chuckling at her for some reason or other, and he enjoyed riling her up about this or that. "Warren!" She would yell, as he would sheepishly hide behind his newspaper. She would then scold him for whatever sin he committed, while he smiled away behind the Mesabi Daily. I'm convinced she was just so in love with him; she could never stay mad and would end up laughing or chuckling as well, at herself and at him.

Yet, Grandma scared me because it was evident that she held high standards she herself met, and she was a strict judge of character. I never wanted her to scold me, I think I would have felt so horrible if she had. I avoided my grandparents during much of my 20's because I was leading a very "colorful" life and I figured they wouldn't be impressed. It would be easier to just show up every now and then and keep everyone guessing.

On one occasion, my parents wanted to get together at the Whistling Bird for dinner with my grandma. The Whistling Bird is in Gilbert, Minnesota, and is one of the nicer restaurants on the Iron

Range. They serve cuisine that is different from your average mom and pop restaurant, and although I love the Iron Range, I will say that they are seriously lacking in fine cuisine choices and places to go that you can dress up a bit for. Anyway, that's where we were all to meet, and in truth, I was only going because Mom and Dad said they would pay for my meal. I was still scared of sitting down with Grandma, but that was probably because I had developed a nasty little liking for cocaine, and I felt like everyone knew I was a great big sinner. I would only do coke on a few weekends when I was bartending and my kids were at my parent's, but the come down sometimes bled into Sunday night and I can't really remember which night this was. In any case, I was looking forward to the food but scared as hell to see Grandma.

If I wanted to meet up with Grandma, I would need to dress in something she would approve of instead of my bartending attire. I had two looks usually. One was hot, slightly revealing and most definitely flirtatious, and the other was tee shirts, jeans, and fuzzy socks. This time I dressed in between. I put on a nice sweater and a pair of jeans without holes. This would satisfy my parents as well, I figured.

As was becoming the norm, I was feeling nervous about being around family, and decided it would be a good idea to arrive early. I would go to the bar nearby the restaurant and order a shot to take the edge off my nerves. There was no way I was going to order the shot at the bar in the restaurant we were going to and risk my grandma seeing her granddaughter throw back like a pirate. It was a perfect plan, and I felt better already.

I drove to Gilbert, which was only about 6 or 7 minutes from my house in Eveleth. My mind had already started messing with me, because I was a bit of a wreck by the time I got there. I had started to worry, wondering if I looked as terrible as I thought I did; my eyes were a bit large in my face and I was aware that I had dark shadows under them due to lack of good quality sleep. I just needed a shot of something and it would be better, I reasoned.

I can't explain why I wasn't fully aware of my surroundings, or why I didn't look up when I came screeching to a halt in front of the bar, but I put 'er in park and hopped out. On the way in, I was digging in my purse to make sure I had my wallet handy and that I had some cash. Sure enough, there was a $20. I should have checked that at home but whatever, I was good for a shot, even two if I liked the first one enough. I went inside and immediately was greeted with a dank darkness that enveloped me from all sides. I walked up to the bar, my eyes a bit spotty due to them taking forever to adjust from the pleasant, sunny, early evening to the dark, inky interior of said establishment. The bartender came over and asked what I wanted.

At this point, I start to feel odd, like something isn't quite right. It's not a fleeting feeling, it stays. Ok, now mind you, the following things happened all within the same 15 seconds:

1. I notice the sultry, sexy music.
2. I can see I'm the only person at the bar and maybe the whole place. (Made sense because it was early, but really? No happy-hour patrons?)
3. The bartender is looking at me expectantly.

4. I hadn't thought of what shot I wanted.

5. There is slinky movement in my peripheral vision to my right.

6. What the fuck bar *is* this??

7. Am I in the **GLADIATOR???** Am I in the only **STRIP** joint on the Range?

"Uh…" I glance quickly to my right. **IS THAT A STRIPPER ON THE STAGE IN ONLY A THONG????** My heart sinks, and I realize I am too far down the main street of Gilbert. I had raced right past the Whistling Bird!

"I'll have a double shot of Jack," I say with false bravado, like I come here all the time. First- gross. Jack is a sipping whiskey and goes best neat in front of a fireplace or on ice with cola while lounging on the deck. No-one but the bad, menacing cowboy in a Western movie wants to slam a shot of Jack Daniels, let alone a double. But here I was, Brave Sara alone in a strip joint called the Gladiator in the early afternoon, about to slam a double Jack. **Why do I do these things?**

Now, I've been to many strip joints in my time, and we all had a great night, but this was different. Going to a strip bar on purpose is different from going there on accident! I wasn't ready! I would like to interject that while I don't take issue with a woman earning her living in whatever way she decides to, I knew that me being in here would go over like a fart in a space suit with my family. It was probably the worst place I could be, in their opinion. I was now a mother, I was supposed to be meeting up with my grandma, and instead, here I was— in the Devil's Den.

With all the courage I could muster, I grabbed the shot glass, put it to my lips, and tipped my head back. I pretended it was water and I was a thirsty dehydrated camel, and I didn't let it pause on my tongue. Let me tell you, I downed that double shot of Jack like I was a pro, ignoring the instant watering of my eyes and the burning in my throat. I then put my twenty-spot on the bar and got up, turning around before I choked. The bartender took it and as he was turned to go get my change, I muttered, "Keep it," like I had so much money to throw around. As he held it up in a salute and nodded his thanks, I started toward the door.

Oh shit, I thought. *What if my parents come down the street with Grandma and my brother in the minivan and see me exiting the **Gladiator**?* To my dismay, I realize there was really nothing I could do about that. I would have to walk out into reality, get in my car and go around the back street to re-approach and park at the restaurant. I'm such an idiot.

I'm sure luck was on my side, because when I left the strip joint, no one was on main street, not a soul. As I drove back out on to the main street a bit later, I saw my parent's van approaching. Feeling relief that I had gotten out of the Gladiator not a moment too soon, I parked my car and pretended I was just arriving in Gilbert. There was little Grandma, all 5'2" of her, dressed up in her sweater, slacks and pearls, diamonds on her fingers and bright lipstick on her lips. What would she think if she knew of the adventure I just had!

"Hello Grandma," I said cheerfully, the Jack now taking effect and warming up my insides, making me feel **nice** and friendly. Maybe a double was the way to go in these situations! I was still smiling as we were led to our table, with Grandma squeezing my hand on the way. *I'll be all right*, I said to myself, *I'll be all right*.

The Girls Slings Drinks

Back in my bartending life, Jackson had asked me out, and we started dating. Fortunately for me, he wasn't a jealous type of person, and he knew I had to flirt at the bar to make tips. I did see my tips decline a little when people found out I was dating someone and I was no longer the single bartender, but I still managed to do ok. My parents would come by every Friday, when my dad was done with work, and pick up Anthony and Chloe. They would bring them back Sunday after church. Usually, I would be getting ready for work when my mom and dad showed up. My shift started at 4 p.m. or 5 p.m., and would end at 2 a.m. It was always my dad picking up the kids, but sometimes it was my mom as well.

They would walk in the door, and I would have the kids ready to go. They had their little backpacks, and I always felt like a shitty mom saying goodbye to them for the weekend. They were already being bounced around between my house and their dad's house, and now my parent's house. Things were not going so great with their dad, and they didn't always end up going there on his weekends, at least not them both. It was hard times for the two little ones, and for me. My mom would always look at me, her eyes going from my face down to my shoes, and her displeasure at my bar outfit was obvious. I'm sure she didn't like my children seeing me in such skimpy attire, but I couldn't help it, I usually had to rush out the door the moment they left. I wish I had known then what I am confident in now. I would have told my children that the body is beautiful thing, and nothing to be ashamed of or hidden. You could dress however you liked, and it only mattered how you judged yourself, and not how others judged you. But, at this time in my life, the burden of guilt was hard to bear, so much in fact, that I was looking for anything that would help me escape this feeling.

The "anything" turned out to be cocaine, like I told you earlier. I wasn't a regular user or anything, just a little bit to get me through some of my weekend shifts. At first, it felt a little glamorous. It was everything fabulous people did in LA. and New York, right? I was getting it for free as well. All I had to do was agree to go to dinner with this guy, I'll call him Mark, and he would toss me a bit of coke. He never tried to sleep with me, he only wanted my company. Now you may be doubting this part but think about it. I have told you so many ridiculous, embarrassing, and slutty things I did, I promise you… if I had slept with him, I would just tell you. Going to dinner with him to the Whistling Bird, having steak and tasting cabernet for the first time, keeping him company, and looking good while I was at it was easy. I also discovered that the drug helped me feel good, and I was even more alluring and flirtatious at work.

By Sunday, I had slept and come down, and although tired and slightly depressed, I was able to parent soberly all week long. Then

Friday would arrive, and I would gear up for another moment of my parent's disapproving, set-jawed expressions. My children sometimes looked a bit sad and forlorn as they left for the weekend. I felt shame that I wasn't leading a life my parents could be proud of, and it ate away at me. It was a lot for me to bear, along with something else. I was now used to feeling like shit as a person. My past abuse took a very permanent place in who I was. I was now my trauma. I had *become* my trauma. I felt toxic, like everything that had happened to me.

Deep down, I felt like one huge loser. I had lost my birth family when I was given up for adoption. I had lost my virginal innocence, I didn't know where that had gone, that part of life was blocked out with the force of a great, iron door. I had lost my chance at going to college because I was bouncing around in California at the time. I had lost my youth along the way, as I diapered babies and tended to the needs of my now ex-husband. I had lost my parent's respect and approval eons earlier. I had lost friends from church, who had long ago distanced themselves from me- the heathen. I lost my baby, due to my inability to provide for the family I already had. I lost my mind for a while I think, brought on by two of my cars being repossessed over the years, and of course, it was men who came and took them. In my warped thinking, it was just another man taking from me, and it triggered all the feelings of men taking from me in the most intimate ways in my youth. I couldn't see the forest for the trees. I was unable to see that with help, I could have lived a very different life, one where I would be able to be so responsible, that no one would take anything from me again.

Bartending was now my best friend and my worst enemy. Oh,

there were nights that it was so much fun, it was like being out, without having to spend money. The bass was always pumping, the lights were flashing, and the fog machine was doing its thing. We would have so many customers, that half-way through the night, we would run out of ice and beer, and the bouncers would have to bring more up. The bar was long, with me working one end, and Kimmy working the other. The bar business in Virginia was booming, and I was lucky to work when it was in its prime. I was making fun drinks and shots, and often would be invited to take a shot with the customers, which Kimmy frowned upon and barely ever allowed. She was small, but mighty, my Kimmy. At the end of the night, we would say goodbye, knowing we would be there tomorrow to do it all again.

Bartending is not for the weak. I took my resentment out by flirting abominably with men and taking them for as much money as I could. They were the fools; I was the smart one this time. I hated that they tried getting some excitement from me, while I knew their wives waited at home. I hated that when I was overweight, none of them noticed me, none of them cared about me as a person, who I was. They only paid attention to me when I was what they wanted me to be aesthetically. This made me hate them even more. In addition to this crap, I had men say all kinds of things to me. They would ask me out, lust after me all night, then get mad when I would not accept their invitations. They would openly talk to their friends in a lascivious manner about my ass, my breasts, whatever they wanted. One conversation went like this:

Dude: "What are you?"

Me: "A girl."

Dude: "Ha-ha... no, I mean, what *are* you."

Me: "What do you mean." (I knew exactly what he meant.)

Dude: "Are you Indian?"

Me: "No. I'm Hispanic."

Dude: "I've never been with an exotic girl before."

Me: "Oh yeah? Bummer."

Dude: "I bet it's wild."

Me: "Guess you'll always wonder."

Dude: "Don't you wanna let me know?"

Me: "Finish your drink and fuck off all the way back to the Mirage where you probably originated." (The Mirage was a really, seedy, off-putting, bottom of the barrel bar just down the block.)

Dude: "Fuck you, bitch. I didn't want you anyway."

Sometimes I would shut them down like what you just read, but most of the time I let them say what they wanted, while I kept taking their money. They were the ones who would go home with whiskey dick, wake up with an empty wallet, and a rip-roaring headache. I would wake up after a long, nice slumber, wads of money, and a clear conscience. Well, aside from the knowledge that I had indulged in a little cocaine. And had not slept that well and would need to drink lots of water and orange juice and would put cold washcloths on my face to bring down the bags under my eyes. Aside from all *that*, I was the better one, right?

As my illustrious bartending career went on, Jackson and I were growing closer, and were pretty much in love. He was a good egg, and I had no problems with him moving in with me. We lived in that little Eveleth house from my first marriage, and things were ok for a while. We had made it through Y2K, and then 9/11. We clung to each other in the living room as the world fell apart that day, and we shared our concern at the uncertainty of the future of our country. We had each other, and at the time, that was enough.

I knew that my parents always hated when I moved in with someone, and with good reason. My kids were being subjected to my crazy, unstable, devil-may-care lifestyle, and it contributed to them not being able to form bonds with people, because the guys I picked never stuck around. Except for Jackson, he stuck around. At the time, I just thought I was getting help in the form of love, friendship, financial help, and a father-figure for them. I couldn't see that it was damaging, because when you're damaged, you cannot decipher and decode damaging choices. Besides, Jackson was good people. He was kind, gentle, funny, and stable.

Unfortunately, I was not used to "kind, gentle, or stable," and had no idea how to handle the boredom it sometimes made me feel. There had to be chaos, right? That is what we were used to. That is what we knew. That is what we understood. We? Who is we? Me; me and my best friend named Trauma. We were in this together!

So, as time went on, I did what I always do, and I sabotaged the entire thing; for surely, I did not deserve Jackson's love. Earlier, on Valentine's Day, he had proposed, and I had accepted, but the ring was returned to him along with promises of a future that could have been wonderful. Looking back, he was exactly what I needed, and had I had help and therapy, I might have been saved from the heartache that was to come.

The Girl Has UPS & Downs

From that last paragraph, you may think that I gracefully ended my relationship with Jackson. I did not. Nope, instead I allowed my head to be turned by a very persistent and flashy package delivery guy. He literally succeeded in getting me to pull over on 5th Avenue in Virginia, with my daughter Chloe in the car, and he asked me out. I said no at first, but he was not used to that, and he persisted. I was pretty sure he knew I had a boyfriend, and I don't think he was fully out of his relationship, but none of that mattered to either of us, because the physical attraction was instant. In the end, I returned the ring to Jackson, and I instead went on this fun, country adventure with Adam Ryan.

 Adam had a truck, and we would bounce along country roads, listening to Brooks and Dunn, stopping every now and then so he could get out and look at wildlife or nature or whatever. I was going through my country music phase, and I played along with this whole country vibe. "Fishin' in the Dark" and "Red Dirt Road" were always playing on the stereo, while the sunset created a pretty picture across the summer sky. I pretended to be interested in fields of grain and wildflowers and summer nights laden with mosquitos, but in truth, I was bored out of my gourd. Yet there I was, being an idiot, leading with hormones and boredom and the desire to be more than what I was.

Adam was outgoing, with a quick smile and cornflower blue eyes that crinkled when he laughed. He was easy to like, and my parents took to him immediately. He was **responsible**, he had a grown-up job and brought a lot to the table by way of provision, and that was something my traditional parents were keen on. It probably looked like we had a great time together as well, as I was caught up in his charm and the way he made me feel safe.

Together, Adam and I were a force to be reckoned with. We were both outgoing and loved a good time, and we didn't really have much to argue about at all. Here was my chance to redeem myself in the eyes of my parents, the community, and even a bit of the church maybe. Growing up the way I did, these things were of utmost importance. I would reinvent myself; I would show everyone that I could do things the right way. I even had a new job, working at the bank. At first, I was a teller, then I moved into customer service. I wore nice, respectable clothes to work, met people from what I thought was an elevated type of lifestyle, and really cleaned up nicely. My partying ways had slowed way down to almost non-existent, and I had done the last of my illegal activities shortly before meeting Adam in the first place. After he came into my life, I knew my wild ways would never fly, he was such a straight arrow. This encouraged *me* to be a straight arrow as well.

Marriage was on the horizon for Adam and me. We also were expecting a child, and I was so excited. We were living in the Eveleth house, and would soon be moving out to Britt, closer to my parents. We had found a little house in the woods, with a big garage and a good-sized yard. We were right where Adam was in all his glory, surrounded by woods and animals and country roads. I would be only 5 minutes from my parents, and being as they were happy with the direction my life was going, this was a good thing. I was beginning to amass what I thought was the perfect storm of life: the handsome husband from a good family, the 2.5 kids, the country home, and a beautiful wedding to start it off.

We were married at the Elks club in Virginia, and it was a great time. I bought him a gun for his wedding gift, can you fucking believe it? ***I had morphed into his lifestyle***, not caring about me or my individuality. In our wedding pictures, you cannot tell that I am seven and half months pregnant. I had willed my body into submission because I loved my wedding dress and it needed to fit. Little Brianna did her duty and hid, and the morning after we were married, my belly sprung to full form, like it knew my dress was no longer going to be an issue.

We lived in Britt for a while, making our home and being a married couple. We were mostly happy, and I can't find much fault with those first years, except one thing. I was living a lie. I had adopted this squeaky-clean image, this dutiful housewife image, this country girl image; I probably deserved an Oscar, or at least a Golden Globe for my acting skills. Oh, I loved my husband, and I loved the way we looked to other people, but deep down, I knew the mask was slipping.

After a year, I could no longer pretend country living was for me, so we moved into a house in Buhl. Buhl wasn't exactly a proper "town," but it did have a post office, a gas station, a few bars, and actual people. Our house was on a big lot, and you could see the highway behind it. It was a nice house, much newer than the Britt country house. Maybe this would make me happy.

At this time, I was able to get my first real glimpse of God working behind the scenes in my life. I had been searching for years for my birth mom but had run into many dead ends. Being placed in adoption was the first trauma in my little life, although I did not know it at the time. God knew it though, and when He started piecing me back together, He started with the first trauma. After years and years of searching, I located my birth mom. I had told myself over the decades of my life that I was fine, and it didn't bother me that much that I was adopted. This was a lie. It bothered me more than I knew, and it had a profound effect on me that I couldn't recognize.

I flew to Texas one April, and met my birth mom and my extended family. For the first time in my life, I felt like I belonged. I felt like I had a glimpse of who I was meant to be, and the life I had lived in Minnesota seemed like a lie, a fairy tale. I was obviously grateful to my mom and dad who adopted me, but now it seemed like the years of "not fitting in" and being "the brown girl" finally made sense. For a brief amount of time, I had a sense of who I was. My birth mom even flew to Minnesota to visit with me and meet everyone. It was during this time that I wrote a blog about my search for her. It was published in the local paper, and I have it featured on my website today. As happy as I was about finding my mother and feeling her love, I also felt more confused than ever about me, my surroundings, and my relationships. None of it seemed real.

As time went on, I felt myself growing restless. I wanted to be me, and my attempts to "right my life" by marrying the perfect guy, having the perfect house, having a "respectable" job… it wasn't conducive to what I really needed. What I really needed, and what nobody told me, was therapy. I needed help. I needed to learn how to rescue myself from my past. I needed to heal the wounds of my past, so that I could be a productive and positive addition to whatever situation I would find myself in.

As it turns out, Adam was less than happy at home, and I was less than happy with him. Whether by feeling me change, or just because he had other things on his mind, my marriage started to do what every other relationship of mine did: it started to crumble. In hindsight, I know I must take at least 50% of the fault of the demise of each of my relationships. What I was bringing to the table was a broken woman-child with too much baggage. In saying that this was 50% my fault, I'm not saying that as a victim of sexual abuse and other abuses that I was intentional in my failings. No one told me, at least, I don't remember anyone telling me, that I needed help. I myself didn't know I needed help, I knew I needed **something**, but I didn't know what it was. So, I would keep searching in every man for the one that would love me for me, and help me, and rescue me. I wish someone had pointed me in the right direction; I wish that if they had, I would have listened. It could be that the people who knew me, knew I wouldn't listen to reason, so they didn't bother trying. I don't know. I wish I had known that I didn't need a man. I wish I had known that with therapy, I could rescue myself and take autonomy over my body, my mind, my life.

After ***almost*** making it to four years, my marriage ended. I felt guilty for my end of it and tried making the divorce proceedings as fair as possible. I didn't want to be the "bitch ex-wife," so I didn't ask for much, and I didn't put up a fight. He was also quite fair, and as divorces go, on paper, this one wasn't too complicated. By now, our daughter Brianna was three years old, and her life was about to change drastically. She was a daddy's girl, and loved the outdoors just like he did. She would follow him around the yard, copying his every move. Anthony and Chloe were older now and had also formed an attachment to Adam. This divorce was difficult for them, because Adam was pretty involved in their lives, he was someone they looked up to. As easy as this divorce was legally, it had a devastating effect on the children. The guilt I felt was instant, but I told myself that if I was happy, they would be happy, eventually.

The timing of the divorce was shitty, just shitty. As luck would have it, right at the end of the marriage and the beginning of the divorce, I almost died. Like, almost died for real. I was at work, driving back to the office from a meeting with a business customer, when out of nowhere, I felt like something was very, very wrong. I was in my car, and fortunately near the hospital, when I felt my insides fill up and a sensation of tearing or pulling. I didn't even debate with myself, but instead drove right to the emergency room. I parked, walked swiftly through the doors, and just about fell over. Someone brought a wheelchair over in lightning-quick fashion, and they were able to catch my fall. I was in and out of consciousness and would wake up on my side on a mobile hospital bed. I was in pain, deep, excruciating pain, and because I kept passing out, I was completely disoriented. I remember being wheeled down the hallway, and the last thing I recall seeing was a big light above my head, and the face of a doctor in scrubs, a mask and an instrument coming at me.

I woke up much later and was brought up to speed on my situation. I had experienced an ectopic pregnancy, and it had burst my fallopian tube. I was bleeding internally and lost quite a bit of blood as a result. Had I arrived at the hospital 20 minutes later, I would have died! As I lay recovering in the hospital bed, my parents were with Anthony and Chloe, and Adam had Brianna. Much later, my dad told me that little Chloe, my tiny 11-year-old Chloe, my sunshine girl, was standing in the hall, looking out the hospital window. My dad asked her what was wrong, (he knew already, but sensed she needed to talk about it) to which she simply replied, "Everything." That broke my heart, and I don't know why he told me that. Maybe he felt I needed to feel more empathy where my children were concerned. Maybe he felt that I needed to know that information, to be a better mother. Maybe he just needed to rid himself of carrying that moment alone, I am not sure. To this very day, I imagine that scene, and I swallow back a lump in my throat, and I am having to remind myself **again**, that I am forgiven, that I am loved, and that I now know **how** to love.

I was now dealing with the loss of **this** child, and even though I had no idea I was pregnant to begin with, it triggered the feelings of the loss of the baby boy I had placed in adoption years prior. In addition, the loss of **this** baby felt like a symbol of my marriage: a tender and beautiful thing that I was incapable of tending to and maintaining. My body was a bit off as well, having an influx of pregnancy hormones and then the slow dumping of said hormones. I was angry that this was happening and hurt by the fact that I was dealing with this alone. Sure, I had my parents, but this divorce was yet another failure on my part, and I felt like the world was spinning, and life was passing me by.

In no time at all, Adam was in a new relationship, and I was living in our Buhl house, which had been awarded to me in our divorce. I had no idea how I thought I would be able to meet my financial obligations, but there I was, living like I had money. I was going out a **lot**, just to feel better about myself. It stung that he had moved on so quickly, and although I didn't want to be with him any longer, it was difficult to see that he most definitely wasn't missing me.

By now, my two children were a bit older, and weren't so needy as they were when they were toddlers. I couldn't see that they still desperately needed their mother, I was too blinded by my own unmet needs. *Fuck it, fuck the entire world,* I thought. I soon went back to my partying ways, determined to be the hottest thing around. No one was going to think Adam made the right choice by moving on right away. Truthfully, I don't think anyone really cared, only me.

24

The Girl & the Crack in the Universe

My parents were helping with things as much as they could. I didn't tell them everything, because I couldn't bear to see their disappointed looks or hear my mother's sighs. Instead, I retreated further into my world of fast friends, fast men, fast times and whatever else that meant. Of course, I did all of this while neglecting the realities of life. I wanted my youth back. I wanted my freedom and a do-over. I was now newly single in a small town, and I was never at a loss for potential dates.

One night out, I met a guy who was with his buddy shooting pool. He was just a really kind dude and although he seemed unassuming and even simple, I realized after chatting with him that he had depth and intelligence that he didn't let everyone see. He was not the type of guy I normally dated, because I normally dated fuckboys and pretty boys. Tommy wasn't unattractive by any means, but he was quiet and not in the "coolest" circles. I decided I didn't care; I was just glad someone was being nice to me and not trying to get in my pants right away. I could tell he was who he said he was; he made no pretense of being anything else.

He and I became serious, and he moved into the Buhl house with me after not much time at all. He had a gaggle of kids, and every other week they were also with us. I didn't bother asking my kids how they felt about this arrangement, I didn't understand how it could be bad, considering I was happy. Also, he was bringing financial help to the table and that's what I needed.

My son was starting to spend more and more time with one of his friends and would go there often or to my parent's house. He would even go to his dad's, with whom he had an on and off relationship with. Instead of seeing this and understanding that he didn't want to be home, I saw this and was relieved that I wasn't having to feed him— he ate so much! If he was happy, that was a good thing, right? ***I didn't even bother asking him if he was happy***.

Chloe was also growing up and was spreading her little wings. She was blossoming right under my nose, but I was so wrapped up in my own hurt, my own losses, and my own unmet needs that I didn't notice this delicate time in her life. I'm afraid much of her time was unmonitored, and a bit unfiltered. She too would go and stay with her friends, and with her dad occasionally. Again, I would be relieved that it meant one more meal that could be spared, because although I was still working at the bank, I didn't make much money at all, and Tommy's contributions were not as much as I would have liked.

Did I say I was working at the bank? I was, until I started messing up. I had checked out and was more interested in running around and being young again. I got called into my boss' office, and I was 1,000% sure she was going to fire me. I would not give her the chance though;

I beat her to the punch and quit instead. So now I was jobless, with a mortgage, a bunch of kids at the house, a boyfriend who didn't have the most upstanding and steady job ever, and no clue what was coming my way.

I was able to get work at the Short Stop just up the street from my house, and although I kind of enjoyed the job, it didn't pay much. But, in the interest of bringing in some money, I had to do **something**, and I didn't need a car to get to work there. I mainly worked weekends, with a few shifts during the week. The girls in Buhl didn't like me much, as I was constantly flirting with all the guys and filling my need for validation by getting their boyfriends to turn their heads. I'm kind of amazed I didn't get my ass kicked.

So, I worked my little part-time job, and on one Monday when I was off, I waited in the house expecting my kids to get off the bus from school. After some time, I realized the time frame for the bus had come and gone, and the kids were nowhere to be found. I was a bit frantic and called Brad to see if he had put them on the bus that morning. He informed me that he did, but that they wouldn't be coming home to me. They all had decided that the kids would move in with him, due to my instability and some other things he suspected about my living situation. I cannot go into these things, as they are hearsay, and the other party is unable to speak to those matters. In any case, Brad put the kids on the phone, and they proceeded to tell me that they weren't coming home.

At that precise moment, I swear the universe cracked in two.

Adam, Brianna's father, had been informed by Brad of my other two children's decision, and he had also informed him of his beliefs that my home was not exactly a safe place. Now, Adam wasn't completely stupid. He wasn't exactly sure he believed what he was being told, because he knew some things that prevented him from taking this information at face value. However, as Brad was talking about getting Child Services involved, Adam felt he should at least check the situation out. He had had Brianna that weekend and called me to let me know he would be keeping her until he could check out these things for himself. He was not unkind when he called me, and he reassured me that Brianna loved me and that it was going to be just fine. I couldn't be upset at him, because he was gentle in his delivery, and he wasn't upset at me. If the universe cracked in two earlier, the echoes of it rang in my ears with this development.

I went into my room, laid on the bed, and sobbed. I sobbed as though my heart had broken, for truly it felt like that was happening. I called my dad and just cried and cried. I remember he listened to me and then told me verses that were meant to reassure me, but I knew I was a rotten mom, a rotten person, a bad daughter, a used up expired piece of shit, and I wasn't good enough to be forgiven or helped. I sobbed for hours; my eyes were almost swollen shut. Never had I ***ever*** had my children's position in my home threatened. Tommy held me as I cried, and we both acknowledged that we needed to get our shit together and get it together ***now***. He would get a real, regular Monday through Friday job, and I would get a job that would pay more, so that we could provide a better place for the kids.

Brianna came home only a few days later in the week, Adam was satisfied that things were on the up and up, and seeing my little girl run toward me filled me with a joy I cannot describe. Yet, Anthony and Chloe had decided to stick it out with their dad, and so my life was not complete, not until they were home. It took one more month for Anthony to decide he wanted to come home, and three months for Chloe. It was difficult for them both to tell their father about their choice to return to me, their mother; it created a wedge between Brad and the kids and myself even, that sadly, would never be fully mended.

I ended up losing our home in Buhl. I was in the middle of trying to sell it, but I wasn't fast enough, and the bank took it back. Tommy and I had been one step ahead and rented an apartment in Eveleth. Tommy got a job as maintenance guy and was able to negotiate a little bit off our rent. I can't remember where I was working at the time. The next month is very blurry in my mind, I think almost losing my kids in the weeks before, and losing my house just made me block out much of the coming months. Of all things to remember, I recall I developed a liking for beer with lemons in it, and I realized that I loved apartment complex living. Everything was neat, compact, and convenient.

In time, in the interest of bringing in a better paycheck, I applied at Delta Airlines, and was granted an interview. Never had I wanted to get hired more than I did where Delta was concerned. The interview came and went, and I got the call - I had been hired! I would start in May! I was so elated; this was a job that would pay decently. We ended up moving to Hibbing which was closer to the Delta Airlines call center. I would be in customer service, as a reservation specialist. Tommy got a job at a manufacturing company in Hibbing, so we were both being responsible adults now.

Tommy and I now had a minivan, which I both loved and hated. It was decent as far as minivans go, but you remember my chapter in Part 1 about minivans, they were very uncool in my opinion. But we had all these kids, mine and his, so we needed a vehicle big enough to get us all around.

Chloe was a teenager, and because she was so outgoing and fun, she made friends quickly in Hibbing. Anthony elected to stay in the Mt. Iron school district and had all but moved in with my parents to keep going there. He would come home on weekends, and sometimes he would go stay with his buddy. He was growing up and would help my dad in the summers. Bri was five and went along with everything cheerfully.

Through the spring and summer and into the next year, I worked at Delta. It turned out that within a month of getting my flight privileges, my grandparents in LA were not doing too well. Because of my job at Delta, my mom was able to fly, for free, to LA just about every other weekend to go and help them. When they passed away, we were all able to fly for free, to LA to attend the funerals and be with family. Even Tommy came with, and I'll always be thankful to Delta for that wonderful gift they gave my family.

25

The Girl & Questionable Happenings

Back at home, things were... weird. The Hibbing house that we lived in, the duplex, was giving off some sinister vibes. The closet in our bedroom always scared me, I felt like it was a portal from the moment we moved in. I was not one to fully **believe** in portals and time travel and such, but this house gave me the creeps sometimes. My dog, Whisper, would bark at the hallway, often-times going over and facing the corner nook that held a few books on it and would yap away. This was kind of unnerving, but not scary. No, there were plenty of other things that could be classified as scary.

Brianna shared her bedroom with Tommy's kids when they came every other weekend. She had a bunk bed in her room, and Addy would sleep on the top, while Brianna and Lizzy slept on the bottom bunk. In the mornings, Addy would come to the kitchen, tired and grumpy. I asked her what was wrong, hadn't she slept well? She looked up at me from under her furrowed brow and said, "No, Brianna and Lizzy kept pulling my blankets off of me." I went to confront the two little ones about this, and they adamantly denied it. This happened a few nights in a row, but each time I asked, they would deny it, and my mother radar determined they were telling the truth. I brushed it off, thinking maybe Addy's blanket had just slipped off while she tossed and turned.

Then, one afternoon, as I was doing laundry downstairs in the basement, Chloe stood at the top and was yelling something down to me. It was just the two of us in the house, everyone else was gone.

Out of the blue, mid-yell, she screamed "**OH MY GOD!**" and came running down the stairs.

"**WHAT?**" I asked, sure that something horrible had happened.

"Someone said something behind me! Like, they whispered!" she said, her face frozen in fear. I was convinced she really was sure she heard something, but I did my best to calm her.

"Chloe," I said, "No-one is in the house but us. The noise was probably the dog, or the wind coming through the windows." She seemed calmer, not entirely convinced, but was able to go about her day, as was I. *Sometimes teenage girls were silly*, I reasoned.

Then, on one quiet evening, I was sitting on my bed going through photos. Tommy was in the living room watching some show, and then he turned the TV off to come and visit with me. Once he was in the room and had sat down on the edge of the bed, we both heard soft footfalls in the living room, which was right off our bedroom. We both sat very still and looked at each other, our eyes wide. Tommy dutifully got up, and quietly stepped out of our room and around the corner to the living area. He came back momentarily and shook his head.

"There's nothing. No one is out there," he said. "I'll go check on the girls." He headed back out of our room and in the direction of their bedroom, which was at the other end of the apartment. I continued to sit on the bed, and softly leafed through the photos in my hand.

Then, suddenly, I heard a very loud whisper right outside my door. "**HEY ADDY!**", it said, the whisper sharp and evil sounding. I dropped my photos and looked up quickly. There was no one there. I froze, and I could hear my heart pounding in my chest. The area where the loud whisper came from, was at the top of the stairs, **where Chloe had been standing when she said she heard someone whisper loudly in her ear!** A few seconds later, Tommy came back from checking on the girls.

"Sound asleep," he said in a normal-sounding voice. "You look really pale, are you ok?", he asked.

I closed the lid on the box of photos I had been looking at just a moment earlier. "Did you talk to the girls at all?" I asked quietly.

"No," Tommy said, then laughed, "you think I want to wake them up once they're asleep?"

"You didn't say, 'HEY ADDY' a bit ago?" Now I sounded a bit hysterical, my voice was quiet, although shrill in tone.

"No, I told you I didn't want to wake the girls," Tommy said, eyebrows raised in a what-the-fuck-is-wrong-with-you expression.

"Well, I just heard a voice whisper '**hey Addy**' so loudly," I said, and by now I was shaking. It wasn't so much the whisper- it was the sound of the whisper. It cut through the stillness of the evening like sharp glass. At this, Tommy at once got all excited, and I knew why. He loved this shit, the paranormal, the spooky and scary things in life.

We didn't talk about it again, but I started feeling not very good about things. I even started to wonder if Tommy was somehow the reason for these strange things that were happening. I knew he loved horror movies and paranormal shows, and now that I was scared, everyone was a suspect. (I roll my eyes here a bit at this part of the story, but at the time, it was truly nerve-racking.)

Just like clockwork, after about one year of marriage to Tommy, it started to fall apart. It was crystal clear to me that I couldn't keep a marriage together. We were obviously seeing things in life differently, and I was starting to outgrow the relationship. It wasn't even that I was miserable, it was more… a case of knowing this wasn't it for me. I knew this wasn't what was meant for my life. I had always hated living with a guy and not being married. It was ingrained in my mind and told to me throughout my youth, that living with a man without being married was a sin. It was wrong. So, to right the wrongs, I would agree to marry them. Oh, it did occur to me that leaving a marriage was probably also a sin, but I felt like I was choosing the lesser of two evils. I chuckle a bit now, of all the sins I tried to fix, marriage was the one I was most concerned with.

Tommy was understandably not pleased, but he was kind to the end. He moved out of our little duplex and into his own apartment, and wouldn't you know it… the energy in the home changed. In fact, a friend of mine came over, who had been at the house many times before.

"Did you paint in here?", she asked.

"No," I said, looking around the room.

"Huh, it seems warmer. Like you painted with a warm color or something. Odd," she continued, sipping her coffee.

Well, isn't that interesting, I thought, noticing that the house had indeed seemed to warm up, and the feelings of dread were gone. Now I'm not saying this was Tommy's fault, I'm just saying things were different when he left.

The Girl & a Daughter's Wish

By now, I had quit Delta because it was too intense for me. I couldn't deal with people yelling at me on the phone all day about the weather and flight delays. I couldn't stand the demanding, condescending tone of the silver medallion and the gold medallion flyers. I couldn't stand the prices of tickets and I would try and sell people the lowest fares I could find. I got creative finding flight times and routing; I just could not stop selling out of my own pocket. This made it so I was on calls longer than I should be, and I would always get warned about it. Also, I detested being micromanaged. I hated it like nothing else. It reminded me of being controlled. The days were long, and one call came right after another, with no time for me to really come down from the previous call before I was expected to take the next one. So, after months of trying to stick it out, I quit.

I was tired- so fucking tired. I had tried seeing a therapist a few times during the last years, but they always wanted me to talk, and I wasn't ready to talk about the mess that my life was. I was raising my children by myself. Anthony was too grown up now, I felt like I had missed out on things and didn't even know him anymore. He was a good kid, quiet and tall, handsome and kind, my gentle giant. Yet, as much as I loved him and knew he loved me too, I couldn't tell you his favorite color, or his favorite food.

Chloe was beautiful, and she had a boyfriend now. She was flitting here and there, living her little life like it was one big adventure. It was no longer cool to hang around mom, she would rather be with her friends wearing too much makeup, singing songs at the top of their lungs, and having sleepovers. Because I was tired, I let her be free, after all, isn't this exactly what I had wanted as a teenage girl— my freedom? I didn't say no to many things- if she was honest with me and didn't disrespect me. Sometimes that happened, sometimes it didn't, but I was too tired to have the energy to deal with it when it didn't. Plus, I loved her so much, and felt guilty telling her no.

Brianna was my wild child. She was energetic and bright; she always doing something. I suppose because I was a bit older when I had her, I was more attentive in my job of raising her. Her dad, Adam, was single again, because the woman he had been in a relationship with right after me, ended up breaking things off with him. They had a little boy of their own, (fuck my life) so he was Brianna's half-brother. Brianna was devastated when they broke up, because every other weekend that she would go stay with her dad, she would spend time with Kristen and her little brother. She was very worried that Kristen no longer loved her, and although I reassured her that that simply wasn't true, she could not be convinced otherwise.

I hated the idea of Kristen. Back when Adam and I were over, she was the first person he had a relationship with, like, the ink was barely dry on our divorce. I had seen her maybe once or twice but made it an absolute certainty that I didn't have to see her more than necessary. Because she was working at the same place he had been when they met, I wanted nothing to do with her. I couldn't deny that she was good to Brianna though, so I never uttered an unkind or jealous word about her, especially around Bri. Bri had a right to love her, and I would never take that away from her, no matter how bitter I felt. So, while seeing my daughter's tears, I asked her if she would like me to call Kristen, so that she could see her again. This immediately cheered Bri up, (*you've got to be kidding me*, I thought) and so I placed a call to my old boss, Kimmy.

"You two would really get along, if you would just talk and get to know each other," Kimmy had told me at one time, laughter in her voice. I might have told her to fuck off, there was absolutely no way I wanted to get to know this person; now here I was, being forced by the universe to get in touch with her. Kimmy didn't need to say anything, her laughter said it all. She passed my number on to Kristen, and I waited to hear back. I brought Bri to Walmart with me while I waited, and passed the time looking at things I couldn't really afford. Kristen ended up texting me first, asking if she could call me in a few minutes. *Why not*, I thought ruefully, but instead I agreed and pretended I was totally cool with it.

When she did call, I don't remember much about that conversation except that I found myself really enjoying her voice, and the things she had to say. She would come and pick up BriBri (Kristen called Brianna "BriBri") and take her to the park. I was just happy my child was going to be reassured that Kristen would always love her. Bri hummed happily while she got dressed to go, and I forced a bright smile to encourage her happy demeanor.

Kristen showed up right on time, and Bri bounded ahead of me as she ran to the door. Out she went, and straight over to Kristen's arms. I couldn't help the real smile that formed on my face, my daughter was so happy. Kristen said hello and assured me that she would bring BriBri back soon. I watched as they drove away, and I went back in the house, not really knowing what to do with myself.

I cleaned. I counted down minutes. I wondered if I should invite her in when they got back. I had spent so many years hating the idea of facing her, and now here it was, the moment I was dreading. I felt nervous but calm at the same time. The ex-wife and the girlfriend-turned-ex-girlfriend meeting on the common ground of our love for BriBri was happening. What would I do with this moment?

Sure enough, they returned within the hour, and before I had a chance to make up my mind, Brianna invited Kristen in the house. Kristen looked at me to make sure it was ok, and I found myself welcoming her in, almost obediently.

What happened next was the beginning of the first real "mature love" relationship I ever had, the first one that I was able to maintain and take care of. No, not in **that** way, but in a way that only two people with a child between them **could** love each other. We chatted into the late afternoon, laughing at similarities and fact checking timelines and moments. We understood why he had fallen in love with each of us, we were so similar! She was the organic version of me, and I was the devil-may-care version of her. We joked that had we smooshed us together, we would be the most perfect woman alive.

I ended up inviting Kristen back the following weekend for some real fun. She knew nothing about wine drinking, she drank beer I think, and whatever else. I had just discovered Lambrusco while I was perusing the liquor store down the street. It was cheap, it came in a big bottle, and it tasted pretty good, so that was a plus. I felt extremely sophisticated, holding my glass full of red wine-juice. I had forgotten that Mark had introduced me to a decidedly more sophisticated Cabernet back in my bartending career. I didn't know yet that Lambrusco was kind of the bottom of the barrel, thanks to the history of the 70's and 80's and the watering down and misrepresentation it received over time. No, instead I was walking proudly around my apartment, wine glass in hand, pretending I was fabulous.

Kristen and I went out on the town when she came back to Hibbing. Bri and Leevi (Kristen's son with Adam) were at their dad's, so it was just us. We got ready at my place, hit a bar called The Brickyard, and had an absolute blast! I didn't know life could be so much fun, until l hung out with another version of myself. I don't even know if The Brickyard was hopping that night, because Kristen and I discovered that we could be anywhere and have the time of our lives. We were single, we were full of laughs, we were all dolled up, and we didn't need anyone but each other.

Men would naturally flock to us because our positive energy was so infectious. Kristen and I were physically opposite. I was dark haired, dark eyed, hourglass shaped and not afraid to be bold. She was willowy, light skinned and light haired, green eyes, and came across as shy in her manner. Together, we were the perfect blend, and that explained why we got so much attention in those early days. We used to get a kick out of guys coming up to us, because it was always the same. First, they would come up all smiles, and just kind of stand there looking from one of us to the other. I know how stupid that sounds, but I'm telling you, that is what happened, and often. Second, they would introduce themselves and ask our names. Third, they would ask how we know each other, because "you two look like you have way too much fun!" She would look at me, I would look at her, and we would break into a knowing smile. Kristen usually spoke up because I never could get it right.

"That's my bestie," she would say, "she's my son's half-sister's mom." By this time in the night, when guys got the courage to come up to us, they were a bit tipsy, as were we. When you're a bit tipsy and you're hearing this riddle of an introduction, the fourth step in the process was inevitable. This is where we would do a countdown in our heads, looking at each other, silently counting down, and waiting. They would stand there, confused looks on their faces, sometimes a pointer-finger up in the air that would go from me to her and then back to me. Every now and then, they got it, and would say something along the lines of, "That's really cool!" A few guys actually just turned around and walked away. Whether it was because it was too much for them to process, or they wanted no part in whatever witchcraft was happening at our table, I don't know, but we would always erupt in laughter.

I was still getting into a bit of behind-the-scenes trouble, mostly just guys and stupid decisions. I was not indulging in illegal substances or anything, but I was definitely drinking too much wine on the weekends, then over-exercising and under-eating. I was enjoying being free and everything that entailed. Once again, I felt myself sort of escaping into the joys of freedom because my children were older, and Bri was going to her dad's every other weekend. My job at Caribou was meeting the rent because I was working five or six days a week and had been promoted as well. Things were going well, and I felt like I wasn't a total shit person.

Kristen and I would spend as much time together as we could, sometimes getting our children together, and sometimes just us. The first time I met her family, it was on the day of her son's birthday party. I had to explain my friendship with her to my parents, because I'm pretty sure they were confused. I had thus far painted a negative picture of her, and now, all of a sudden, we were best friends. I sheepishly told them about our friendship, and although they weren't upset about it, they were skeptical. This went both ways. Kristen also had to explain our friendship to her parents as well, as I was probably not presented in the best light at first. I'm not sure what was said to them about me prior, and it doesn't matter now anyway.

I showed up to Leevi's birthday party, gift in hand, and tried to put my nerves away. Many of the birthday guests were her family; I would be meeting her parents for the first time, so I tried to be on my best behavior. I didn't know anyone there except Kristen, so looking back, I'm kind of impressed with myself and my moxie! I walked in and it seemed like the whole room looked my way. I smiled, and they cautiously smiled back. Pretty soon, we were visiting and laughing and having a good time, and I knew that I had found good people. I think they liked me as well, and they must have been able to see the chemistry that Kristen's and my friendship had. From then on, we were even thicker than thieves.

We didn't talk about Adam that much. We were so into each other, that the past didn't matter, rather, it was merely a funny and absurd time that brought us together. My hurt at the fact that Adam divorced me started to dissipate. Even though I wanted to be free, it still hurt that he was the one who filed, he beat me to it damn it, and I was embarrassed. Yet, somehow, my friendship with Kristen helped heal that hurt and embarrassment.

The Iron Range in northern Minnesota is a small place, everyone knows everyone's business. My divorce with Adam and his relationship with Kristen immediately after were two very well-known events that I'm sure welcomed gossip and rumors. Many people were confused at our friendship, but we didn't care. We knew the truth of the timing, the events, and the reasons why, and that is what mattered. If we were good with things, the rest of the world would just have to deal with our friendship.

The Girl, An Old Flame, & the Sister Wife

I was still living in Hibbing, I was working at Caribou Coffee, and I was feeling pretty good. My shifts at Caribou started at 5:30 a.m. and went until about 1:30 p.m. This was great because I was home every afternoon and night with the kids. On one afternoon, I was in my room, laying across my bed and scrolling Facebook. I saw I had a message and friend request from a familiar face— Brandon Davies, from California! He was one of the boys from around the block back in Concord, a former best friend of my ex-boyfriend's! Just seeing his face on my phone screen, all the memories came tumbling back. He had grown up; he was a total man now. Gone was the awkwardness of high school and early college, and in its place was a grown-up. I couldn't deny my attraction to who he had become, and I welcomed his message and friend request.

It didn't take long for us to realize that the attraction was mutual, and because of our history, our love story took off like a shot. We were calling and messaging often, and exchanging updated photos and moments in our lives as they were now. We agreed to be exclusive, and I felt very happy.

I was still spending time with Kristen, but now I wasn't on the prowl. I had Brandon, and I was so excited, because he was going to come and visit! He would fly into Duluth, and we would stay there one night and then come back to Hibbing. The one thing about Brandon that I adored was that he was fun, an optimist, and even though I had so much trauma, I was an optimist as well. Or maybe I was just in denial, I don't know, but together we were two very fucking annoyingly happy people. The cup was always half-full, and there was never a shortage of laughter between us. He understood me, and sometimes he would tell me things that he remembered about when I lived in California. Most of his memories were only his, I had blocked out so much of my life there that I couldn't conjure up some of the things he would talk about. I felt great regret and frustration with my inability to recall things, and at once I knew my trauma had had a profound effect on me. However, I wasn't ready to deal with that yet, so instead, I lived with my frustration and would soak up the memories he would tell me. Side note: living with constant frustration is not recommended.

Brandon stayed with me about a week, and we talked about everything. He had once rescued me from a very, very traumatizing, and horrible incident that I can't even speak of, and I owed him so much. My kids liked sharing their lives with him, too, especially Anthony and Bri. I believe this was because Anthony had such a tumultuous relationship with his own dad, and Brandon was someone he could look up to. Bri was very attached to me, so anyone I loved, she loved. Chloe was polite, and thought he was nice, but she seemed to hang back a little, her trust in my decision-making was probably shattered. Chloe's star was shining brightly, but from a different corner of the universe. It was one that I had a difficult time reaching, but I loved her fiercely, so I kept trying. I thought Brandon would be the thing that our little broken family needed, and he was, until I fucked that up, too.

Sometime that summer, Brandon and I decided that I should move out to California to be with him. First, I needed permission from Brianna's dad to move her out of state. That would be a hard sell, so I tried to think of ways I could make it an easy choice for him. I told him he could have her for the summers, and that I would be responsible for her airfare each way. I said that I would lower child support, and even bring her home over Christmases so she could see him. He seemed to be agreeable to this arrangement, although he may remember this differently than I. I can't speak for him, I will only say that my lease was coming up on my apartment, and I felt comfortable enough to inform my landlord and my boss at Caribou that I would be moving. My little Caribou family even gave me a going away party! I was so excited about my return to California with my kids. Chloe would do her senior year out there, and I was excited for her. I can't remember a time when I asked her if she was excited or not. I was so used to fulfilling my own needs, that I often didn't consider the needs of the people who were supposed to be the most important in my life.

I took the girls, and we went out to visit Brandon at the house he was renting specifically for us as a family. I don't know where I got the money to do this, taxes maybe? Or perhaps Brandon helped me, I can't recall. It was also decided that Chloe would stay in California, so that she could start school while I finished up in Minnesota. I didn't want her to have to move in the middle of her senior year, I thought it would be easier to just start her fresh on the first day.

We flew out together, and our dog Whisper came with us. I would leave Whisper with her, so that she would have a bit of home to comfort her if she felt lonely. "***If*** she felt lonely..." because I had the ability to detach from people emotionally rather easily, I didn't even think twice about the very real possibility that Chloe needed her mother. I never really needed mine growing up, or so I thought. I forgot about my big search for my birth mom, I forgot how it felt to be loved and nurtured. The abuse I went through allowed me to turn emotions off like a light switch, I was in constant survival mode.

I came back home with Brianna, and I had a rummage sale to get rid of all my possessions. I would not need them for the move, only our clothes, I reasoned. Then, Bri's dad started to question my intentions more and rescinded his initial agreement. He wanted things to go through court, and he told me I would need a judge's permission to move with Bri. I felt completely unprepared, and gob smacked. I had already given my notice to move and had quit my job! I was panicking, and I was also furious. As a more mature person, looking back, **he was right** to want to secure these things in court, I just wish he had said that from the beginning.

Thankfully, Kristen and I were still as close as two friends could be, and she kindly offered to let us move in with her while we figured it all out, ***if*** we figured it out. Talk about a relief! I thankfully moved myself and Bri to Kristen's Virginia home, and humbly accepted her offer to let us stay in the downstairs bedroom next to Leevi's. Brianna and I were so close, she was mama's girl now. We shared a bedroom and life was pretty good, considering the situation I was in.

Our living arrangement was probably the most fun, happy, and pleasant situation I had found myself in, in a very long time, if ever. I contributed what I could at first, and I very quickly got my bartending job back at The Sports Palace which allowed me to contribute a bit more. Kristen was going to school at the time, and every now and then, I would watch her little boy for her during the day. What a turn-around! Years before, when I was divorcing Adam, the idea of getting back together was presented to me, and I had said, "I'm sorry, I could never. There's no way I want to see her kid when he comes to visit you every other weekend. I don't have it in me to deal with that." Now, here I was, loving that little boy and even babysitting him for Kristen. Funny how time and friendship and letting go of one's ego seems to heal wounds.

My first day of babysitting Leevi, he must have been about three at the time, maybe a little older. Anyway, Kristen gave me strict instructions that he was not to have any gum. She kind of stressed this to me over and over, in a few different ways. Ok, I thought, kind of odd thing to have to worry about, but maybe he was a little gum enjoyer and couldn't keep it in his mouth. I imagined it on furniture and chairs, and maybe even in his hair. *Alrighty, no gum*, I thought. Kristen had been gone not even half an hour, when I noticed that my little charge was not anywhere that I could see him. I laughed and started playing hide and seek, thinking he must be trying to trick me.

"Oh! I wonder where Leevi is," I said loudly, wandering around the living room. "Hmmm," I continued. "I will look downstairs!" I went down to his playroom and bedroom, but no Leevi. I came back up, still talking out loud and looking. I checked the bathroom and Kristen's bedroom, to no avail. Finally, I looked behind the cushy chair in the living room, and who did I see, but a little boy, his tufts of blond hair sticking up like Calvin from Calvin and Hobbes, his cheeks rosy, and his big green eyes staring up at me in wide-eyed anticipation. I took one look at his full cheeks, and I just **knew** he had not one, but several pieces of gum in his mouth. *Fuck*, I thought, *now I must get him to give me the gum*.

"Leevi," I said. "Are you chewing gum?" He looked at me, mouth closed tight, and didn't make a sound or a movement.

"Leevi," I continued, "you know you're not supposed to have gum. Your mom said so, now please, give me the gum." I put my hand out so he could plop it in my palm, but he sat there, mouth pressed in a firm line. By this time, I was starting to sweat. This wasn't my kid, and I couldn't very well yell at him. I didn't want to get forceful; this was the first time I was watching him for Kristen, and I didn't want to cross any lines. I could feel my face getting warm from my inner turmoil. Now that we were at standstill, I had to establish the hierarchy here, or he would never listen to me.

I tried one more time. "Leevi, you need to give me the gum, right now." I held my hand out again and tried to look serious. Once again, he firmed up his mouth, but had the decency to look down this time. To my absolute horror, and probably his as well, I reached out, put my thumb on one side of his cheeks and my middle finger on the other side, gave a gentle but firm massage and press, and his jaw opened wide. I reached in quickly with my other hand and retrieved the gum.

"Thank you," I said in a way too-pleasant voice that bordered on hysteria. I don't know who was more horrified and shocked at this point- Leevi or me. I went and threw the gum away, and then came back with a book. I would read to the little punk because I think we both needed to be soothed. He willingly sat next to me so he could look at the book while I read, and he seemed to have a new sense of obedience about him. From that horrible day forward, we had good days, and no more battles of wills, thank God.

Things were great between me and Kristen. We started calling ourselves "sister wives," due to the unusual situation we found ourselves in. We thought it was funny, because we each had been in a relationship with Adam, we each had a child with him, and instead of hating on each other or disliking each other, we basically were now married to each other! We lived together, ate together, laughed together, co-parented together, and enjoyed wine together.

Our wine tasting became more expansive, and we graduated from Lambrusco to Cabernet, Merlot, and Tempranillo. We were drinking so much wine, that instead of putting our bottles out for recycling, we just put them in boxes and hauled them to the recycling center ourselves. There was no need to let the neighbors know the extent of our indulging. We had arranged for Adam to take the kids on the same weekend, which worked out nicely for us all. We had plenty of weekends to play; when the kids were home during the week, we would sit together in the kitchen after they went to bed and share a bottle (or two) of wine while we would catch up from the day.

I was still in a relationship with Brandon, and we would text and talk often. Chloe was starting school, and I missed her so much. Brandon was true to his word, taking care of her and our dog Whisper. I was trying to find a lawyer I could afford, so that I could get everything in writing. I knew it was either going to be a smooth transaction, or a battle, one of the two. I didn't have the financial means to go head-to-head with Adam in court over Bri's move to California, so I was trying to get him to agree outside of that, and just have it be a matter of paperwork being signed by a judge. This was not proving to be easy, and time started to march by. I was frustrated and afraid I wouldn't be able to move after all. I was annoyed at myself for sending Chloe out there so soon. *I should have waited*, I thought.

Brandon was good about calling and texting me, and he was truly in love with me in a way that I found easy and comforting. I loved him back, but I was still me, not yet evolved. I had tried seeking therapy like I stated earlier, but I would always quit when they wanted to start digging into my past too much. I was still a broken person, and every good situation or relationship was merely a Band-Aid solution for a bunch of gashes and broken bones. I didn't know that until I addressed the trauma that held me captive, I was going to fail at every relationship I took part in. Any will or gumption I possessed was going into the kids, and working enough so I could provide. Brandon put me on his phone plan, or I probably wouldn't have been able to afford the monthly upkeep on that either.

Kristen was also bartending now at The Sports Palace where I was working. In addition, I had taken an easy job cleaning The Magic Bar on Saturday and Sunday mornings. The owner was a good friend of mine, and I knew he didn't really need me, but he hired me anyway and I pretended not to know he was being charitable. When I wasn't working at The Sports Palace, I was bartending at Wink's bar down the street. It sounds like we were working all the time, but in truth it was not every weekend night, and we did have plenty of opportunities to go out ourselves. We would have a grand old time, drinking, flirting with guys, doing the countdown, and enjoying our friendship.

One night we went out, got way too tipsy for our own good, and found ourselves separated. It wasn't a big deal because it was Virginia, and nothing really happened in Virginia. I ended up walking back to her house, all alone. I probably shouldn't have been crossing the highway in the shape I was in, but I managed to make it safely. (Thank you, Jesus.) I swear, my guardian angel was working over-time up until this point and was probably asking God why He had assigned them to me.

Once I got to her house, I realized I didn't have a key to get in. Thankfully we were having a "second summer" so the temps were still warm. I decided to lay on my back on her deck and look up at the stars. There I was, enjoying the quietness and the bright twinkling show above my head, not knowing that somewhere across town was my equally tipsy Kristen, cursing me out in her mind because she thought I had left and taken off with some random. Eventually she came stumbling up the walk, and upon seeing me laying on her deck, she burst into giggles.

"Wiiiiife! You're here!" she exclaimed, her hand reaching out for the railing as she teetered on her high heels.

"It's meeee!" I sang, sitting up slowly to prevent the dizziness from happening. "I'm here."

"Ah!" Kristen said in a bright voice, as she took a seat beside me. She looked over at me and smiled. "My friend! … I thought you left me!"

"No silly," I assured her as I sloppily patted her leg. "I thought **you** left **me**! Then I got here and didn't have keys!"

That said, we both got up and Kristen proceeded to unlock the door, giggling away as she swung the door open. I started laughing also because everything was always funny as long as we were together. We got inside and started unpeeling the night off us.

You see, when I moved in with Kristen, I was still very much about my looks. I wouldn't be caught dead leaving the house looking less than perfect. It was my shield, if you looked good, no one could tear you down or take advantage of you. I was also very straightforward and not too gentle in my delivery of things. I tended to be over-confident (probably to make up for the insecure way I felt inside) and for this reason, I didn't have many friends. Girls didn't like me. I think they found me arrogant and lofty. Being this way was my protection, my defense mechanism. No one would challenge me if I was too intimidating or scary to approach. So it was that I found myself marveling at how **nice** Kristen was. I would be talking shit about someone, being blunt about their shortcomings or something they said, and Kristen would say in her sweet and kind voice, "Well, maybe they didn't mean it quite like that…" and she would go on to help me look at people in a new way, a kinder way, a gentler way. Maybe not everyone was a jerk, maybe some people, like me, were just misunderstood.

In return, I brought Kristen into the bathroom, and had her sit down. Kristen is a very earthy and organic girl; she never wore much makeup at all. She didn't do much with her hair, and I didn't understand that. If I had her body and her bone structure, I would be simply unbearable to be around. I introduced her to fake eyelashes, hairspray, curling irons, makeup, and even pretty piercings. I felt like it was an even trade. She would make me nice, and I would make her pretty. Now when we went out on the town, it was almost perfect. I had no idea that people, (women in particular,) could be just fine how they were.

28

The Girl, the Ghosts, & The Golden Boy

Many months before, when I had first started visiting Kristen at her Virginia house prior to moving in, I was chatting it up with her while she was making a Mac and Cheese lunch for Leevi. As we were talking, I stood in the entry way to the living room, where I had a clear view of the kitchen and yet wasn't in the way. Something caught my eye and made me look up just in time to see a black mass move along the wall and float down the hall. Now, let me just tell you that it wasn't dark out by any means. This was not a shadow and light chase that you might see when a car comes down the street at night and their headlights make odd shadows in your home. There was not smoke from anything she was cooking, and a big bird didn't fly by outside or anything. No, this was all on its own, and was not flat **against** the wall, but rather was in the air **next** to the wall. I froze, and just sat there quietly, debating on saying anything. Kristen's mom was also there visiting, and, as I didn't want her to freak out, I kept my mouth shut.

Later that day, I quietly told Kristen about what I saw. If I expected her to be alarmed, I was to be disappointed.

"Oh yeah," she said as she washed the dishes from lunch. "My mom's seen that too, same area of the house! Pretty sure my house is haunted." I stood there with my mouth agape, and then thought, *oh well, I guess if she's not worried, I don't need to be.* I closed my mouth and proceeded to dry the dishes.

Shortly after that discussion, I moved in with her, and the memory of the black mass was long gone. Once I moved in, she would tell me stories about the things she saw in the house that were weird, and instead of being scared, I was more intrigued than anything, and kind of thought maybe she was imagining things. Or at least I figured she was exaggerating a little bit. Either way, I wasn't too worried about it at all.

One late evening, after an uneventful and rather boring night out in V-town (Virginia, to the layperson), we decided to just drink some wine and visit at home. It was cheaper and way more fun than this evening out. Nights on the Iron Range can be like that: one weekend it will be hopping, and everyone is out, and other nights, it's like someone is having a big garage party that you aren't invited to, rendering the downtown bars almost completely empty. This was one such night.

Now I told you a few paragraphs ago that I was drying the dishes. That's because although Kristen had a dishwasher, we never used it, because it never worked. It wasn't a big deal for me to wash dishes in the sink because my duplex in Hibbing didn't have a dishwasher. So, her dishwasher just sat there, serving no real purpose to anyone. Besides, it was old anyway and probably didn't do too thorough a job.

There we were, sitting at her table in the small dining area adjacent to the kitchen, around 1 in the morning, when unexpectedly, Kristen stopped mid-sentence.

"Do you hear that?", she asked, her pointer finger up in the air. I sat still and cocked my head, listening. I shrugged and looked at her. "That," she continued, jabbing her finger in the direction of the kitchen. "Is that the **dishwasher**?" I slowly turned my head and sure enough, I could hear the whoosh, whoosh of the water in the dishwasher, churning and swishing around pleasantly. At once, Kristen hopped off her chair and went into the kitchen. Sure enough, that old thing was busy going at it, washing nothing. Now the curious thing about her dishwasher was that because it was so ancient, it didn't have anything digital on it; it still had the old-fashioned knob that you had to use a little bit of force with to turn in the correct direction to make it click and turn on. Not only that, but it would make a sound when you turned it, very much like winding something up. I watched as Kristen turned it off, and then slowly walked back to the table. We both just looked at each other for a pregnant moment, and then started laughing. What else could we do really? Maybe it was just one of those things, we reasoned, **maybe**.

Another night, Kristen was working at the bar, and I was home. I don't know why I wasn't out that night, maybe by then I had no other friends besides her, who knows. It was getting late and although I was tired, I also wanted to visit when she got home and have a bit of wine. I decided to lay on the couch and wait instead of going down to my room. I laid there, drowsy, when I heard the sliding glass door click and start to slide open. I sat up, thinking she was home. I had a clear view of the slider, but there was nobody there. I listened, but there was no sound. Confused, I got up and went to the door. It was closed but unlocked. I started feeling a bit spooked, so I quickly locked the door and went back to the couch. When Kristen got home, I mentioned the door and that I thought I heard it open. She nodded.

"Oh yeah, that's happened to me a few times. I would go to bed, and then hear the sliding glass door click and open. I would be sure I had locked it, but when I would get up, it was unlocked." She poured herself a glass of wine and joined me on the couch. "I started closing it with purpose and saying, 'lock' out loud, so that I knew I was really locking it. It didn't matter. So many times, I would get up and it would be unlocked." She took a long sip of wine and smiled. "Welcome to my world," she said. "Aren't you glad you moved in?"

We went out the next weekend we had off, both of us agreeing that we needed to get out of the house. We went to BG's, a kind of dive bar that was the favorite of so many locals, where the burgers and wings were some of the best around. We grabbed a corner table and made ourselves comfortable. Within what seemed like only minutes, we were joined by a guy that I can only say looked like fun, and trouble, lots of trouble. He had a charming, mischievous smile that reminded me of the little boy in A River Runs Through it, the one who played a young Brad Pitt. I hate even mentioning that because he loves when people compare the younger him to Brad Pitt. He eats it up and I feel my eyes rolling to the back of my head.

Kristen introduced me to Jaden and the sparks were instant; it was like meeting the male version of myself. I had a false sense of importance at this time in my life, so you can imagine what kind of a fucked-up situation ***that*** was. If I was fire, Jaden was gasoline. To Kristen's credit, she did warn me about him, once, and I ignored her. She mentioned that he was a bit of a free spirit and was just coming out of a relationship. Never mind the fact that I was still in a monogamous relationship with Brandon in California. My loyalty had never really been tested the way it was with Jaden.

My phone calls with Brandon were getting less lengthy, and sometimes I would miss a call here and there altogether. Usually that was because I was busy enjoying my freedom. I hadn't been this free in years. I was always living with a guy or at least in a relationship that was physically right in my face. Brandon wasn't right in my face, so it gave me plenty of time to do what I wanted. In the months before, Kristen and I had gone to California for a visit and stayed with Brandon. We had so much fun, doing this and that, going here and there. Kristen really liked Brandon and I was glad she approved. So, when I started texting with Jaden, she wasn't thrilled at first, but, in true Kristen fashion, she never judged me. She knew it was difficult maintaining a long-distance relationship and understood that I was also a free spirit.

Jaden texted me one late afternoon and told me I should come over and visit. He lived within a stone's throw of Kristen's house, which made it too easy to say yes. Kristen was out that same night, maybe on a date or something. Brianna and Leevi were at their dad's, and I had the night free. Like an idiot, there I went, over to Jaden's to "visit." Brandon called me, or rather, I called him, so that I could get the mandatory phone call out of the way and not worry about him calling while I was visiting some guy I had just met.

I'll pause the story to tell you that I am not going to blame every bad decision on my trauma per se. In writing this, I have lost count of the phrases: "due to my trauma," "because of my inability to" and "I was incapable" … I will reference the following excerpt instead:

(April Goff, Hypersexuality [sic] and Sex Repulsion, September 29, 2021, fortraumasurvivors.com)

"In a person with trauma, there are many reasons for this [hypersexual] activity. Some of these reasons may, unfortunately, cause them harm. They may feel that sex is "all they are good for". They may feel a desire to retraumatize [sic] themselves. Going along with this, they may seek out rougher and more traumatizing sexual activity. Sex may become a part of how they define themselves - including that they may see themself [sic] as an object. If they were traumatized by someone who they believe cared about them, they may feel that sex is the best (or only) way to feel cared for again. They may believe that pleasing someone else sexually is the best way for them to feel loved or valued. Some people may dissociate during sexual activity. Hypersexuality [sic] may cause them to deny parts of who they are."

I know now that trauma legitimately rewires the brain. It changes the way the brain receives information and the way it translates said information. You could say I was stuck in a prison of my own making at this point. I was in fight or flight mode since I was a child, and for me, flight mode involved escaping the realities of life by whatever means necessary, including sex. Back to the story…

There I was, sitting on Jaden's couch- laughing and talking, when suddenly, I found myself being swept up in a kiss that up until that time, I can only say should be in a reference book somewhere that defines the 10 best kisses in all of the world. There was just no coming back from that kiss; I knew it, Jaden knew it. I went home after that kiss, my head scrambled and my heart racing. The right thing to do, would have been for me to call Brandon in California immediately, apologize to him, and never see Jaden again. As you probably know by now, I wasn't keen on doing the right thing when it came to my love life.

Over the next weeks, Jaden and I were spotted everywhere, laughing, flirting, and drawing eyes no matter where we went. We didn't publicly display affection, because I was not being honest with Brandon, and as far as Facebook went, I was in a relationship with him still. Also, as far as Brandon knew, I was just out having fun. He knew I was friends with Jaden, but he trusted me, and I took advantage of that. This sucks to write. I worry at this stage if my readers are tired of me… but this is my story, and the truth of who I was. Jaden liked who I was, he thought I was a blast. I liked who he was as well, I thought he was hilarious, and we got along like a house on fire. People would ask us if we were together, and we would say no, but our eyes and our body language would beg to differ. We were like best friends, bouncing around Virginia and Mt. Iron, leaving fire in our wakes.

By this time, poor Kristen had all but given up trying to be the angel on my shoulder, and instead, joined in on the fun and we became like the Three Musketeers. We would go out and have a grand time, and there was no shortage of things we would get up to. Jaden had an adoration for a good Bloody Mary, so we ended up learning how to make those very well. Jaden also enjoyed cooking, so we invented "Thursday night dinners," where we would congregate at either our house or Jaden's house and cook up a storm. We would invite other people as well, but it was our party, and we had a lot of fun coming up with cooking ideas.

I referred to Jaden as "The Golden Boy" because he had blond hair and blue eyes. He was like the sun to me, and I was all about fire and sun. As time marched on, it became apparent to us both that this was going somewhere fast. I would need to come clean with Brandon. I reasoned with myself that it was the long distance that was difficult for me, and nothing more. The stress of trying to get Adam to agree to let Bri move was becoming a lot to deal with, and he had all but said no by this point. I would need to send for Chloe and bring her home to me.

Brandon was furious with me when I told him the truth of the situation with Jaden, and rightly so. Chloe flew home, and by that time, I was living with Jaden. We had turned a downstairs room into a bedroom for her, but she was not thrilled. I couldn't think about that too much, I felt very guilty as it was. I had really wanted this to be the last relationship for me because I was so in love with Jaden, so blinded by his sun I was. What I didn't know, was that Jaden had his own things to deal with, and maturity wasn't one of them. He had a bit of a wandering eye, and over time, I would be clued in on that.

I was working at AT&T, no longer bartending, and I was bringing in a decent paycheck. While I was living at Jaden's, Kristen had moved to the Twin Cities area of Minnesota. Now she was about three and a half hours away. Our close friendship took a pause because of both of our moves. At AT&T, I was learning all about phones, how they work, and a lot of tips and tricks. This came in handy when it came to exploring Jaden's phone while he slept.

It turned out, my light didn't seem to shine bright for him any longer, but I know now that that was due to him getting in his own way about so many things. He had his own set of issues, and at the time, he lacked the maturity to have the adult relationship I was craving. There were moments and things on his phone that I found to be a direct insult to our relationship, and the way we started out did not lend itself to trust anyway. I shouldn't have been surprised, because as it was, I was having a tough time dealing with some of the things that he brought to the relationship from a previous relationship, and those things were making it almost impossible for me to feel sane at times.

On one occasion, an incident occurred that proved to be the final straw for me where his past was concerned. We had been out on Thanksgiving morning, at Flaimer's bar having one Bloody Mary—just one. Now, I can drink way more than one Bloody Mary before I feel silly, so the alcohol was not a factor this day. We got home, and when confronted with the issue at hand, I lost it. The last thing I remember, was throwing a clock on the floor. The **next** thing I remember, was that it was approximately an hour later, and I was in the bathroom, sitting on the toilet seat. The house was in disarray, and

Kristen, who was home for the holidays, was crouched next to me, asking me if I was ok. Jaden's parents were there, and a phone call was placed to my parents as well. Apparently, I had lost the plot for an entire hour.

I had been pushed so far concerning this issue, which I cannot speak about because it involves people who are unable to defend themselves or speak for themselves. It would feel wrong to give the details of that moment, but I **can** say that I do feel justified in the fact that I could bear it no longer. This situation was directed at me maliciously over and over; I had reached my breaking point, and I snapped. Speaking of "snapped," are you familiar with that TV show? The one on Oxygen, about women who just finally had enough and committed a crime? Yes, that was how I felt. I completely blocked out that hour of time, but the way I behaved caused enough concern that people came to help Jaden get me calmed down. I now understand how people can claim "temporary insanity" when they are up against charges. I used to think that was all bullshit, but I'm here to tell you that I left the stage for a while and have no recollection of the events that happened while I was gone.

Because Jaden knew that this situation was partly his fault, due to him wanting to avoid conflict and not putting a stop to the cruel things that were directed my way, he advocated for me to stay with him and he would take care of me, instead of maybe any alternative that involved doctors. One by one, the concerned parental units left, as did Kristen, and it was just Jaden and I left. I cried for what felt like hours; big, crocodile tears slid down my face, as I was faced with the reality of the previous moments in time. It was **scary** to lose time like that. And although I had not physically harmed Jaden in any way, I felt horrible for losing utter control of my actions. I felt shame, just like I had time after time when I was released from a moment of abuse. To Jaden's credit, he held me and comforted me, and acknowledged his contribution to my breakdown. I knew then that we were over. We had become a storm that was too much for even us to control.

To distract from the events of the late afternoon, we got in the car, and drove to Walmart, 25 minutes away. As we drove, we listened to music. The song "Say Something I'm Giving Up On You" was playing, and as I looked out the window into the night, two giant tears slid down my face. I was sad. Sad because I had gotten myself into this mess, **another** mess with a guy. Sad because my kids would end up suffering because of my lack of wherewithal to get it together. Sad because my heart ached for Jaden's sole loyalty and love. Sad because I had thrown Brandon's love away. Sad for the wasted time, and the realization that the issue that led to this malfunction in my life was probably never going to go away, it would always be there. Sad because I could see the finish line off in the distance between The Golden Boy and myself; it was only a matter of time.

The final blow to our relationship would come that spring. Kristen had been staying in Elk River with relatives and was moving to a more permanent place in Plymouth. Plymouth was about 15 minutes from Minneapolis proper; it was a beautiful, busy, and progressive suburb. I had planned on going down to the metro and helping her with the move. She was hauling things down from her house in Virginia, and it was my chance to get away from Jaden and my now tumultuous living situation.

The trust between he and I was completely broken, in reality- it was non-existent. As it turned out, it was a chance for him to be free of me, and he did what he did with that chance. Helping Kristen with her move involved me and Brianna going down on a Friday night and helping her family unload the moving truck. I found out that same evening that Jaden was up to no good in my absence. Saturday morning, I drove my truck back up to Virginia, and while Jaden slept off the previous night's activities, I packed up my belongings in my truck, all by myself. I had left Brianna in Plymouth with Kristen, who had once again come to my rescue. I would move in with her, because there was nothing left for me at home with Jaden.

Goodbye, Golden Boy.

The Girl & the Playing Field

The first few months living in Plymouth were good for me, yet they were some of the worst times as well. I was very broken about losing my Golden Boy and spent many nights crying into my pillow over the whole thing. I had loved him so much, and I had wanted it to work so badly. He was the first boy I had been with that somehow remained just out of reach. I suppose that was what I found so appealing about him. He was the impossible love, manifested in this blue-eyed, blond-haired, good-natured guy that could make you feel like you were the best in the world, and then the next second, he was done, and another girl was pregnant. I was so broken, my stomach hurt constantly, and it took everything I had to put on a happy face for Brianna's sake.

Because of my previous experience and a glowing recommendation from my former boss at the Hibbing Caribou, I was hired at Caribou in Plymouth. I started work at the Lunds & Byerlys location, where I was the only employee on during the day. It was a little kiosk in the upscale grocery chain, and I liked working alone. I would get there very early and would be done by early afternoon. Bri would stay at the apartment with Kristen, because at the time, Kristen was on midnights. It worked out nicely because Bri would sleep in, and I would leave her something to eat when she got up. Then I would be home a few hours later, and we would have the whole rest of the day together. Being in a new location helped with my sadness, because although I never had any extra money, I had the sunshine, the city, and my daughter.

Chloe was up north still, having graduated by now and was living with a friend of hers. I had wanted her to come with me, but she liked it up north and wanted to stay in the area. Also, I think she was just done with my moving around. In addition, she had met someone, and that was also a tie to the Iron Range. I missed her so much, but I understood.

Anthony was at my parents, he was working at Target and going to school. He had started college a year later than the kids in his class, as he was busy working and figuring it all out. I missed him, too. I tried to keep our communication always open and would get to see the kids when I would go up north to visit with my parents. Because I made the effort to check in with them more regularly, we grew closer and closer.

I lived with Kristen for about three months. I was saving up money because my apartment was going to be available in August. Kristen was on the ground floor, and I would be on the third floor, directly above her.

Once again living with the wife, and probably because I chopped my long hair off, my parents thought that perhaps I was gay, and that she was my lover. I could see why they thought that. We were constantly calling each other "wife" and we were always together. In fact, the entire apartment complex thought we were gay. We heard later that when we would go walking across the quad with our kids, they would say, "There go the lesbians in 109." I laugh at this because maybe life would have been easier if we were a couple! But, alas, we were not. We had taken the dating world on by storm. We both discovered Tinder, Plenty of Fish, and Bumble. I may have been sad because of my breakup with Jaden, but I wasn't dead yet; I was sure my guy was out there somewhere. Gotta hand it to me, I never gave up on love, despite of my not being able to maintain a relationship.

I ended up going on many dates, once with a prosecutor for the state of Minnesota - I don't think I measured up to the kind of woman he was expected to date, because although it was a good date, we only went out once. He took me out to sushi at Chino Latino in Uptown, when he brought me back to my apartment complex, he could see I lived with a roommate and didn't even have my own place. I think that went over like a lead balloon. *Oh well,* I thought, *he's just not my person.*

The next person I dated was a guy I'll call Alex. He met me down the street at Jake's (where I met most of my dates) and we had a drink outside in the patio bar. He was ok, but extremely full of himself. He kept talking about his boat on Lake Minnetonka. He was so pleased with himself, I didn't have the heart to tell him that I grew up on a private lake, I hated it, and disliked spending my day on the water. Instead, I let him try and impress me and I danced around answering his invitations to spend the next weekend on his boat with him. He worked for American Express, and he let me know that he could get us into just about any party, and there were never any shortages of perks that went along with his job. I was bored out of my mind because we talked about nothing of substance.

Then I met Rich. Rich was actually a nice guy, a genuinely nice person. He had a child, which I wasn't thrilled about; his kid was younger than Brianna and I felt like I had just started to again enjoy my freedom because she didn't require much maintenance. In any case, I agreed to go out with him, because he was so nice. While I waited for Friday to come around, I met another guy on Tinder named Eric. Eric was **Gorgeous** with a capital G. He looked like a model, and I was immediately ok with it. He asked me out as well, and I couldn't believe my lucky stars. He was only available Friday, but I had already booked my dinner with Rich. This meant I had to do the abominable: I stacked my dates. I decided I would meet up with Eric for drinks. Everyone knows the one you meet up with at the **end** of the night for drinks, was the one you wouldn't mind maybe having a bit of a lustful tryst with.

Friday finally rolled around, and Rich came to pick me up. He showed up nicely dressed, and, knowing that I was fond of wine, he even brought me a bottle. I felt a bit bad because I knew I was going to ditch him shortly after dinner. What made it a little easier, though, was that I discovered that he fudged his height. On his Tinder profile, he said he was 5'9". I'm kind of an expert when it comes to judging people's height. If there is a robbery at a gas station, you best hope I'm in the vicinity because I'll be able to tell the cops the exact height of a person rushing out the door, and I'll only be off by a millimeter or two. When Rich walked in the door to pick me up, I knew **instantly** that he was 5'8" on a ***good*** day. I will clarify right here and now, that although I tended to like guys that are taller, I would most ***definitely*** date a dude who was 5'8" or shorter if there was stimulating conversation and good chemistry. I just didn't want to be lied to. Don't lie. I hate that. I can lie, but no one else can do that sort of thing. In truth, I think I just wanted to justify my shitty decision to stack dates.

We went to The Sunshine Factory and had dinner, and then after some visiting, I informed him that I had to go. He was a bit disappointed, but he was friendly and a good sport about it. I felt a twinge of guilt as I got out of his car and walked in the direction of my door. I walked slowly, and when I was sure he had gone, I went over to my vehicle and got in. I was going to go meet up with Eric, and maybe get my groove on. He was so hot, and my ego needed a pick me up after the whole mess with Jaden.

I was to meet Eric at the hotel across the street. They had a bar, and we would sit there and have a few drinks. I was ridiculously excited, and when I walked into the bar area, I looked around for model-man. I didn't see him right away, but that didn't worry me. I was a titch early. I would just sit down and wait. While I sat on a seat in the lounge, I heard a voice from directly across.

"Sarita, it's me, Eric." I looked up. There was a guy, who had been sitting there all along. I didn't notice him- because he was unnoticeable. He kind of blended into the couch, his jacket was the same shade of green that the chaise was, same fabric and everything. But more alarming than that, was that the guy who claimed to be model-man, only bore of slight, albeit ***distant*** resemblance to the man in the Tinder app. Same full lips and light green eyes, but he was decidedly way out of shape, and not the v-cut dude I had chosen to go out with. I mean, that would have been totally ok, had he told me upfront or not put a picture on his dating profile that made his current looks unable to connect. It wasn't just this alone. No, Eric had not only misrepresented his body type, but also his height. His Tinder profile said he was 5'11". It was obvious to me that Eric was 5'9". The cherry on this sundae was that he was also covered in moles. Not just a mole or two or three or even four, but rather it was like a congregation of moles came to hold court on his face and body.

Now, I am not a "10." I don't claim to be, and I'm ok with not being a 10. Some people may find me attractive, and some people might not. **At the time**, I was shallow as fuck, not going to lie. I may have even shot above my station when it came to some dudes. I just didn't want to be **lied** to. **Don't lie to me!** I don't like surprises, and I dislike misrepresentation. It triggers things for me that lead back to being assaulted and taken unawares. I can deal with the truth of things, but I cannot deal with a lie. If Eric had been honest in his profile, I may or may not have dated him. At that time in my life, I probably wouldn't have, only because of the mole situation. Like I stated earlier, I was quite superficial in those days. I realize he couldn't help the company of moles he was keeping. I also understand that I have a larger nose and a smaller chin and stick out ears. You don't have to date me, it's fine, but I will give you the choice of deciding before I reel you in with a photo that has been totally altered.

Immediately I wanted to go home, and I was kicking myself for bailing on Rich for this situation. I didn't want to appear to be rude, however, so I made a bit of small talk with Eric, and finally let him know that this wasn't going to happen. Although he seemed pretty disappointed, he leaned in for a kiss before I left, and I was blown away by his breath. It was not good, and I instantly stepped back. He looked hurt, and I felt like an asshole. It was difficult for me to say no, and so, like an idiot, I let him kiss me. I felt like I could feel my very being shrivel up very much like the shoes of the Wicked Witch of the West in The Wizard of Oz. I should have said no, but my boundaries were kind of non-existent. I cut the kiss as short as I dared and got in my truck. I left the parking lot, and Eric, in my rear-view mirror, as I headed home.

Once home, I was frustrated to find that Kristen had gone to sleep already, as had Bri, and I didn't have a key. I had to sneak into the complex quad, and knock on the sliding glass door to get in. I don't know if it was Bri or Kristen that got up, but I slunk in the house like the loser I felt I was. I never stacked dates again after that, and I trusted Tinder way less.

Turns out, I wouldn't have to play the dating field much longer. In an odd turn of events, California Brandon and I reconnected. It was good talking with him again, it felt like home. He had had ample time to recover and heal from our last go-round, and I was eager to have him put me out of my guilty misery. I apologized over and over for cheating on him with Jaden, and I really meant it. I felt bad, and I welcomed the chance to do it right this time.

We fell into a good, solid, respectful relationship. I minded my p's and q's and was on my best behavior. In addition, I was now in my own apartment. Bri and I had moved upstairs, and we were enjoying all the mother-daughter time in the world. I wasn't distracted by men and my unresolved need for sexual attention, so I could instead give her all my time and energy, the way it should have been all along.

I had made a circle of friends, who also lived in the same apartment complex as Kristen and me. Many nights us girls would meet in the quad, and while our kids all played together, we would have drinks and grill. We would sit out there until evening, and then we would all go back to our apartments and put our kids in front of a movie, while we visited and had cocktails into the wee hours.

It was a good time in life, even if my financial situation was not desirable. Oh, we somehow scraped by, I was able to pay my rent and feed Bri, but there was not much money for anything extra. Sometimes I would go to the food shelf, and Bri thought it was so cool that we were getting "all this food for free!" I didn't have the heart to break it down for her, so I let her think we lived a good life. We even started going to a church I had found. It was so different to the church I was used to. People seemed happy to be there, and that was a new thing for me. They sang out, and sang loud, and they had a band and lights that just helped to celebrate Jesus. You could say that I was on my way to better moments possibly.

Brandon came out to visit, and he met all my friends. They liked him right away, and it was so good to see him again. We made plans, and this time, he would try and come to Minnesota to live. He had a son who was one year older than Bri, so Brandon would try and go through the courts to be able to move with him, being as the mother wasn't really in the picture in a favorable way. We were so excited about our plans, and Brandon even looked in to working for Hennepin County, because he worked for the county in California. Things were taking a positive turn, and I was in love again.

The Girl & Karma's Visit

There I was, clinging to my young daughter's love, my long-distance boyfriend, and all the sunny days Minnesota offers up in the summer. I was working at Comcast now, and not only that, but my son Anthony had moved in with me! I was so happy. I had persuaded him to move to the metro, transferring to the Target store here, because there were so many more opportunities for advancement down this way for him. He would go to school at the U, work, and live with me until he figured out where he would go. I was employed at Comcast, and Anthony or Kristen could watch Bri while I worked. When I would get home, Anthony and I would sit together and have a glass of Maker's Mark and talk about our day. These were good days. Anthony and I really got to know each other and enjoy our mother-son relationship that we sort of missed out on as he was growing up.

Brandon and I were not doing so well, however. Now it was I who would call him, only to get his voicemail. My texts would sometimes go unanswered for hours. I went on Facebook and saw that he had given a birthday party for his son, and there were a few photos of the event. Curious, and kind of drawn by intuition, I looked at the comments.

There was nothing odd, except, one comment stuck out to me more than the others. Oh, it wasn't flirty or anything, but something about it gave me pause. The commenter was a woman, and I had to creep on her Facebook profile. She was the polar-opposite of me. Tall, dirty blonde hair, and athletic, kind of like a woman you might think could play football, like… a safety on the defense. I was brunette, short, small, and if you put me on a football field, I would probably start cheering, or more likely, I would run away. Suspiciously, I started combing through his posts, and found other comments or photos she had liked, and I knew. I just knew.

I was desperate to save my relationship and protect what was mine, but to no avail. He finally told me about her, and what could I say, I had it coming. Turns out, she was a big personality out in California, a DJ for one of the hottest radios, one that I used to listen to, and she had quite a following. Brandon had not only traded me in, he for sure had upgraded. There was no way I could even compete with what she brought to the table career-wise. There they were with VIP passes to Jingle Ball. There they were going to her family cabin in Tahoe. There they were attending parties that only her radio connections would allow. It wasn't a smooth time, and there were many heated exchanges between me and Brandon. I even sent her screenshots of the conversations Brandon and I had, with the intent of informing her that he already had someone he made promises to; she was getting involved with a man who was supposed to be involved with me. Turns out, she didn't give a shit, in fact, she blocked me. I probably seemed crazy to her, and who knows what he told her, but I was furious and for the longest time, I couldn't bring myself to ever listen to any Northern California radio stations, in case I heard her voice.

I was sick. I was mad; mad at him, mad at her, and mad at myself. In Brandon's defense, I don't think he ever intended to do this to me. I really don't. I think… with the long distance, and the court proceedings that were not on his side, and the blowback from the mother of his child, he just didn't have it in him to fight for us any longer. How could I not understand? With that reality in the forefront of my mind, I picked up the pieces and went on, like I always do.

The Girl Gets Schooled on Grief

During this time, I tried therapy again. I probably just wanted someone to listen to me talk about my current situation and how "unfair" it was. One of my friends was on an anti-depressant that was working wonders for her, so I went in to see what could be done about me.

The first visit in therapy was always the part I found annoying. You don't get help that day, you must inform the therapist about your life and what you need help with. It was the same story every time I would switch therapists. I would tell them that growing up, I was sexually abused, (I would leave the rapes out because that was too personal) and eventually I was both physically abused and emotionally abused as well. I would say that I was not able to maintain a relationship, and that I was probably depressed. I almost had a whole quick speech made by then, I had been to therapy so many times.

The second visit, we would start talking about how I felt about life in the present. The therapist probably wanted a handle on how badly my life was being affected by my past. Mostly they would just listen, writing notes the entire time.

The third visit would usually consist of going back to childhood, and what things I felt in relation to that. I would talk about being adopted, about being the only brown girl in the area I lived in, and all those things I disliked about being me. Still, the therapist would take notes and ask questions, which I would dutifully answer with my usual answers. I was used to this routine; I had done it so many times.

The fourth visit is where I would start to pull away because it would get uncomfortable. I detest crying in front of people I don't know, I detested crying, period. In the fourth visit, the therapist would start to want me to talk about my past abuse. This would trigger such feelings in me, and I would sit there trying to figure out a way to talk about things without crying. Up until this time in my life, even my friends didn't see me cry, ever. If I cried about anything, it was usually at night, into my pillow, or maybe the shower.

During this fourth visit, my therapist told me that she suspected I was grieving. *Grieving what*, I thought. I didn't have to ask, though. I was told that I was probably grieving my innocence, my youth, and what could have been. I was given a pamphlet about the stages of grief:

- Shock
- Denial
- Anger
- Bargaining
- Depression
- Acceptance and hope

- Processing grief

The therapist told me that it would seem like I had gone through shock and denial already, denial manifesting in the way I had been living my life: carefree and what some might call "selfishly." She said that Anger, Bargaining and Depression sometimes roll into one giant emotion for people, or switch back and forth between the three. I was probably now in the depression stage, where things felt like they would never change, and I was hopeless. I mean, she wasn't wrong about that. I did feel sad and depressed these days, as I watched my youth slipping away, and with it, any chance at really living life the way I wanted to—happy and free from the pain and anger I carried with me.

I listened dutifully, even contritely, all the while planning my escape from having to deal with the muchness of my life. On the third visit, she had reached out to my doctor and recommend an anti-depressant. I had gotten what I came for. It was just the talking that I didn't like. I sometimes felt like my brain would freeze up and I couldn't recall things, or I couldn't bring myself to talk about them out loud. The words would not come out of my mouth, literally they would not. I would even press my lips together, an unconscious reaction to the idea of speaking of my trauma.

On the day before my fifth visit, I canceled all my appointments and stayed home instead, in the safety of the walls around me, and the people in my life who didn't bother me about my past. *I will just change things on my own*, I thought. I knew that I needed to get it together, I could do that. I **would** do that, for real this time; for Brianna, for Chloe, for Anthony, and for me.

Healing

A Different Kind of Love, Mate

After Brandon, all during the holiday season, I had a lump in my throat. My heart hurt still, but I was able to find it in me to try and live my life happily. I found myself bouncing back rather quickly, maybe because I was used to relationships not working out, who knows.

My son was still living with me, thank God. I think he was a bit of a life saver, in that his cheerful disposition really did help me heal my wounds. My daughter Chloe was now in a committed relationship, and she had given birth to my first grandson. She and I had started our own healing journey, and we both tried to forgive me, and mend things that needed mending. I loved her fiercely, and I started seeing it didn't matter my reasons ***why*** I made the choices I made where she and Anthony were concerned. Up until that previous summer, I had always had an answer for why I did the things I did. The turning point for Chloe and I was when I was ready to put my reasons aside and acknowledge the fact that my choices had hurt her. I had to apologize for things and tell her that I was sorry for causing her pain and throw my excuses and my reasons out the door. It was then that forgiveness started to make its way to the surface, and we began to heal.

It was late January, and I was going through Tinder out of sheer boredom. I was absentmindedly swiping, kind of on autopilot. I had the presence of mind to be aware that everything I had tried doing up until this point was not working. I had promised myself that I would make changes. I needed to do something different. I stopped swiping, went to my settings, and changed the age range of men I would be willing to date. Gone were the 30-something year olds. I slid the age bar from one year younger than me, to about five years older than me. I must let you know that this act was a huge deal for someone like me. My Latina roots gave me younger looking skin, and my immaturity helped me pass for much younger than I was. I could pull guys in their 20's even. Yet, now, I knew that if wanted to break the unhealthy cycle I had going, I needed to date an adult.

I also changed up my profile bio. I removed everything that shouted, "a wild time," and instead wrote something about being a Christian, and wanting to include God in my life, which by this time in my life, was not untrue. That ought to get rid of a lot of noise, I mused, smiling ruefully. I had never dated an actual man before, except for maybe Brandon; otherwise, I dated mostly dudes and guys. You ladies know what I'm talking about. I hoped that by changing up my bio and my age preferences, I would find someone that would be responsible, fun, and would like me for me. I was older, I was tired, and this was kind of a last-ditch effort.

Sure enough, there was a picture of a man who looked mature, kind, and even **fun**. He had an awesome dog, a big old brindle dog with a large head. His bio seemed like he was a normal person, someone I wouldn't have to worry about going on a date with and ending up in a jar in a warehouse. So, I swiped right. Immediately, the screen changed, and Tinder announced, "It's a Match!" That meant he had already seen my photo and my bio, and had swiped right on me, too. For those of you who don't know, swiping right on someone's Tinder profile meant you were interested. Swiping left meant you were not interested, and the next candidate would appear on your screen. We had matched, though, so I supposed that was a good thing.

I think it was only a matter of minutes before I got my first message from Devante. You can message within the app, and he reached out and said hello. We started chatting, and I found out he was from Australia. I've never had a desire to learn about Australia, so that detail left me unfazed. He was Chilean, in fact, that's where his family originated. The idea that he was a Chilean Australian, who spoke English with an Aussie accent, but could also speak fluent Spanish, made me laugh. I had to hear it, and so he called me. As soon as I answered, I started laughing. He was a good sport and laughed along with me.

At first, I had trouble understanding everything he said. I had never heard someone speak with an Australian accent in real life, and he spoke quickly. What's more, he had odd words for things, like… he called the trunk of the car "the boot." He would also say things like "air con" or "lift," which were the air conditioning and the elevator. A baby buggy was a "pram," there were just so many things that were different, but I caught on quickly.

We talked for hours, and there was never a shortage of subjects to explore. He was extremely intellectual, and for the first time in my entire life, I found myself struggling to keep up with conversation, but in a good way! Usually, because of my parent's insistence that us kids read books and didn't watch a lot of TV, I would find myself beyond conversations with guys. They just couldn't match my vocabulary and the ease with which I could formulate words and thoughts. That isn't a brag, it's just the reality of what it was.

Devante and I texted and talked on the phone constantly, and in no time at all, we decided it was time to meet in person. I had him come to Plymouth; I didn't know that at the time, it was a big ask. Devante rarely left his neighborhood, he had everything there. Plymouth was about 15 minutes from Minneapolis proper, and to him, it seemed like the ends of the earth. Plus, he was from Sydney, so suburbia was not really on his radar. Nevertheless, he came to me, and we met at Jake's. I was a little embarrassed, the staff at Jake's probably was used to seeing me meet my dates here. They probably assumed I was an escort of some kind. I'm surprised they didn't shake up a dirty martini the moment I walked in the door.

I arrived at Jake's and walked in, he had texted me and told me he had gotten us a table. I was wearing a pair of skinny jeans, black boots with a small heel, a black and gray tee shirt with a Captain America shield done in black on the front, and a long black sweater. I felt a bit like a ninja, and slinky like a cat. Devante saw me and stood up, and his face broke out in a smile. I smiled back, and all at once, I knew it would be ok. We sat next to each other at dinner, instead of sitting across from each other. We chatted and chatted, never running out of things to discuss. We talked politics, no one had ever talked with me about importance of programs, education, healthcare, or world leaders like Devante did. I kept abreast of things and had my beliefs, but none of my friends or previous boyfriends seemed interested in that world, so I had no one to talk to about it.

After dinner, when we could no longer sit and hold the table hostage, we decided to go back to his place and continue visiting. For the first time, going back to his place didn't necessarily include physicality. We were truly enjoying each other's company. So we went, and instead of going to his loft, we went to the rooftop deck of his building. His apartment building seemed exceptionally grand, with chandeliers and big columns and beautiful floors. We got in the elevator and whooshed up to the top, where he brought me to the space that overlooked all of Minneapolis. It was quite a sight. It was then that I felt my heart drop a bit. It was evident that he did decently for himself. There was no way I could ever afford this type of a place. For the first time in my life, I questioned my humble little apartment and my beat up green truck. Yet, that went out of my mind for the time being, because Devante was kind, and good, and after a bit of time just visiting, I was on my way home, my heart happy.

It was late, and as I quietly turned the key to my apartment, I was startled to see Anthony sitting on the couch.

"Anth!" I said, "You're still up!" I had figured he would have gone to bed; I knew Bri was already sleeping in my bed. He looked at me with a slight smile.

"Someone had to wait up for you, make sure you got home ok," he stated. I rolled my eyes, but inside I was thankful for my son. I went to check on Bri, and, satisfied that she was all snug as a bug, I changed out of my going out clothes and put on my pajamas. I joined Anthony in the living room, and we had our traditional little nip of Maker's Mark.

I told him all about Devante, and that I really felt like this could go somewhere, just maybe. As I spoke, I looked around my living room at my second hand, donated furniture. I was well-aware that nothing matched, and my TV was very small by even that day's standards. I had rabbit ears, no cable or streaming even. I had internet because my neighbors were willing to share with me. I was hopeful that this wouldn't matter to Devante, he didn't seem like the type of man that would mind my financial situation, but there was a small chance he was looking for someone as career accomplished as himself.

As I sipped on my bourbon, I wondered if I should even go out with him again, provided he asked. Was it even worth it? Should I just be alone?

I didn't have much time to contemplate it because he did ask me out again. I immediately went down to Kristen's apartment and ran the whole thing by her.

"He's not the type of guy I usually date," I said, being completely real with her.

"That's good!", she said excitedly. "Maybe that is what you need?"

"Yeah," I mused, mulling it over in my mind. "I don't know. He's like… older."

"Sarita, he's your age," Kristen said, laughing.

"Oh yeah," I said, "he's just really intelligent, seems older."

"You have to try everything three times," Kristen reminded me. That was her mantra: try everything three times, from food to experiences and I guess now to dates. I nodded in agreement.

"We do have great conversation," I said, helping myself to a cocktail. "Ok fine. I'll go out with him again."

As it was, I didn't have to date Devante three times to know that this was a good choice for me. It only took one more date, and I was hooked. The real test, though, would be having him over for dinner. He would meet the kids, which was early, but when you know, you know. He accepted my invitation for the following week, and I decided to make Mexican food. It's my go-to when I want to impress. Devante had not had real Mexican food, as there are just not any Mexicans in Australia. Being part Mexican myself, I would jokingly tell him that we can't swim that far… His experience with anything "south of the border" began and ended with Taco Bell. **_Hijole!_** I needed to fix that.

It was with nervous energy that I prepared dinner for Devante. I was mostly concerned about what he would think of my single motherhood, and my little apartment. I knew he would like my kids, how could he not? But I was obviously not living the life he was living, and although I worked at Comcast, I wasn't making a lot of money. I was consistently late on my rent, but it was always paid.

Soon, Devante was at my door, and I let him in with a smile. Bri was excited to meet him, and even Anthony was looking forward to it; or else he was excited about the food, that wouldn't surprise me either. The kids listened intently when Devante talked, I think they were enjoying his Australian accent. He laughed easily, and soon, my trepidation regarding my used furniture and mismatched chairs started to go away. He put us all at ease, when it was us who should have been making **him** comfortable. As the night wore on, he played video games with my son, and I sat watching as they enjoyed each other's company. Bri bounded around the room, peppering Devante with questions, or she would draw something and proudly show him. He gave her his attention, and I smiled and felt like maybe, just maybe, this would work.

I was on cloud nine when I returned to Comcast the next day, and people in my work group noticed. My friend Chaise (who was super fabulous and way too fancy to be working as a customer service rep at Comcast) asked me what Devante did for work. I stopped eating, sandwich paused mid-air.

"You know, I don't know," I said thoughtfully. "I think he mentioned it once, but I can't remember." This was decidedly not good enough for Chaise. He needed details. Obligingly, I texted Devante, and asked him. "Ah," I said to Chaise, "he's a virtualization engineer." I had to Google what that meant. Chaise seemed placated, but then wanted to know where he lived. I think because Chaise saw me as the "older" woman in our group, he felt like he needed to make sure I wasn't doing anything that wasn't benefiting me, or that I wasn't getting the wool pulled over my tired, "granny" eyes. Slightly annoyed, I asked Devante which neighborhood he lived in. He answered me and I relayed it to Chaise. Chaise's eyes got wide, and he picked up one of my potato chips between his long and elegant fingers.

"Girrrrrrl," he purred, with his eyebrows still raised, "you better keep dating him and lock that bitch down honey." I laughed and shook my head. There would be no "locking down" of anything. I wasn't like that. I just knew he was a good man, and I would like to keep seeing him.

Devante was good at dating me. He was aware of my pride and did his best to treat me to things without making me feel like I was incapable of paying, which I was, but he never made me feel as though I was a charity case. He invited Brianna and me over for dinner (Anthony was at work), and we went to his fabulous loft. It was right on Washington Avenue, where everything was happening. The city was alive and there was music and food. His windows were big and even in winter we could hear all the revelers below heading to dinner or their favorite hangout.

Sometimes we would visit him, and he would order takeout, other times, on the nights we didn't have Bri, he would take me out on the town. He loved to eat dinner out, and now that I was in his life, I also got to eat out at restaurants I would otherwise never be able to afford. I couldn't believe this was happening to me, and after many years of bad things, I was thankful for these good moments. We would sit and talk for hours, shutting out the world; it was just us, visiting with each other.

It was usually me going to visit him, because I loved being in the city, and so did Bri. We took her to museums, and places to explore and outdoor patios to eat at. The only thing I hated about going to the city, was driving my forest green GMC stick-shift truck there. It was not nice to look at, and I felt terribly out of place. Usually, I parked on the street behind the apartment complex, and would walk around to the front. I hadn't ever felt embarrassed about my background before, and it would take a good talking to from myself to get that nonsense out of my head. I would just be who I was, in whatever car I had, and if other people didn't like it, they didn't have to look at it.

Everywhere we went, Devante would make friends. People gravitated towards him due to his easy smile and his Australian accent. I felt happy being on his arm and was surprised to feel the occasional pangs of jealousy when other girls would talk to him. He was never disrespectful to me or even to them, and he gave me no reason to doubt his loyalty. Oh, he had baggage he brought to our relationship as well, but over time, and with care, things were put in their proper place.

In the first year of our relationship, I tried going to therapy yet again. I was feeling pretty good, and I thought maybe this time I could deal with things once and for all. I wanted to, because I knew that I had issues with things that I started to notice now that I was maturing and in a stable, healthy relationship. You see, when you're in a healthy environment, it becomes easier to pinpoint the unhealthy things about oneself. In fact, they seem glaringly obvious. Devante encouraged my journey and made no judgements regarding my past. I had finally shared with him about the truth of me: my abuse in childhood, my failed marriages, the son I placed for adoption, and my issues with men and control. He was patient, and kind, and gave me a safe space to confide in. I loved him for that, and appreciated the fact that he never pushed me for anything. He was never jealous, he didn't ask for much, if anything from me. He gave me space when I needed it and was close by when I wanted that.

A few times in our relationship, I questioned God and what He was doing up there. Here was a man that came my way, who I would have probably not dated in my younger days at all. He was stable, mature, financially secure, intelligent, good, and kind. He was sure of who he was and what he brought to the table. It wasn't that I got **bored** with Devante, but I did sometimes feel a restlessness. I questioned it, and wondered if I needed something different. I wondered if I needed a different kind of excitement. I would pray about it and ask for clarification. What should I do?

It was then that I came across an article that talked about the very thing I was experiencing. I read that women who are used to trauma, and the behaviors that manifest as a result, (which then lend to chaotic, unstable environments) often-times struggle at first with normalcy. It feels odd without all the noise from the ups and downs of passion-fueled, sporadic decision making. I would need to re-learn healthy love. I would need to associate love with calmness, peacefulness, void of jumping in on a whim, and never, should I ***ever*** need to fix someone.

I had to learn what many of my former friends who posted their happy family photos on social media seemed to have figured out long ago: **real** love in relationships should be healthy, joyous, and unconditional. I had to learn what it meant to attain that, which I had started to understand with Devante. As for maintaining and retaining, I realized, sadly, that I had no idea how to do the latter two. It took practice to rest in the moments of calmness that were now starting to be a regular part of my life. It took practice to slow down, breathe, and be still in a moment, enjoying the little things in life that I hadn't noticed before. As I tried to do this, over time, it became less awkward and a bit more "normal."

Her Culture, Their New York

Welp, therapy was a bust. I had gone to a few sessions, but when it came to discussing my deepest, most inner thoughts, I once again bailed, and instead kept on with just the anti-depressants. I had been on them before, and when I would start feeling better, I would stop taking them. All throughout life, I found that I detested commitment. I was embarrassed by my former track record with marriage and life, and I found that if I stayed away from commitments, I was ok. I didn't even change my last name when I got married the previous time. I must have known deep down that it wouldn't last.

Anti-depressants did help me feel more regulated and less prone to crying fits and days of feeling blue. I am sure I needed to be on medication, but I also desperately needed therapy, and I couldn't seem to do it, no matter how much I tried. However, with the anti-depressant I was on, I could at least feel like I was leading a somewhat normal life.

I had introduced Devante to my friends by now, and they really liked him, and us, together. They could all see that he was the best thing to happen to me, and with their support, I started to show signs of being able to maintain a relationship. With Devante, I found myself wanting to be kind and helpful. I found myself **choosing** to be less selfish and less of a wild child. I didn't have the wandering eye I was so used to having, probably because my emotional needs were being well taken care of.

Devante and I had been seeing each other for about a year when he moved in fully. He never pressured me about marriage, knowing I had an aversion to it from the beginning. Anthony had moved out of my apartment in the months prior, and had moved into his own place, and Bri welcomed Devante into our lives. He used to call her his "Bri-lee" because he introduced her to martial arts movies and shortly after, she took up Tae Kwon Do. The two of them would kind of "gang up" on me, teasing me and having secret laughs between them. I would act annoyed, but we all secretly loved it. It was like we were like a real family.

I was working at a credit card processing company, and I had weekends off. It was a regular Monday through Friday work week, and things in life were, for the first time, peaceful. Oh, Devante and I had our arguments every now and then. However, they were so few and far between, that Brianna would often-times worry when we did argue, because it wasn't the norm. I had to always reassure her that we were just arguing, and everything would be ok. I found myself arguing differently than I used to. I valued Devante's opinion of me, so I hated if I ever "lost it" when we argued. To avoid that, I started to make sure and think about things before they just went flying out of my mouth.

Devante was also very instrumental in teaching me about my culture. Since he came from a Latino background, he knew so much about things I had never heard of, and I listened with rapture. We shared feelings about being Latinos who happened to be American. He would play his Mexican or Spanish music often, and I found myself getting familiar with the words and the music. He knew I had been raised in a home that was unquestionably "white," and that my experiences with my own culture were very limited. He encouraged me to take pride in being Mexican, Spanish, and Cuban, and soon I started craving my culture and wanted to learn everything there was to know. Previously, growing up in Northern Minnesota, I had wanted to **hide** my brown skin. I had wanted to blend in with the Finnish girls and the Swedish girls and the Norwegian girls. Yet, with Devante's influence and encouragement, I started being proud that I was brown and proud of the cultures I was a part of.

Another cool thing was that Devante's mom in Australia would call him just about every other night. He would put her on speaker, and they would speak Spanish to each other. I started to pick up the language and what was being said, and I figured I should tell him I understood much of it- in case anyone needed to say anything they might not like me hearing. He laughed good-naturedly and assured me that it was fine, and encouraged my pronouncing of words I would try out.

Devante's mother Magaly was kind and loving toward him, and toward me as well! When she was younger, she was a wow, but she was also ***muy política***, very political. Back in Chile, she was member of a political party that protested for the rights of the people. She would often find herself in protests where it got quite heated with the government. Sometimes this would include tear gas, and Molotov cocktails; in fact, she would occasionally be guilty of throwing them herself, or picking up and throwing back canisters of tear gas. She was a strong woman before that term started getting tossed around as liberally as it is today. She always believed in justice and equal opportunity, especially for women, and had instilled those beliefs in Devante throughout his young life. I couldn't wait to meet her, and I was trying to learn Spanish better so she and I could visit, as her English was not her preferred language.

Because of Magaly, Devante understood the single mother that I was. He understood the pride I had and the need to feel like I was taking care of my daughter and myself. Devante also felt it was his job to help take care of me in whatever way I allowed. Devante's mother had taught him to speak up on behalf of women and their rights and their abilities. I owed so much to this woman I only ever saw on FaceTime or in pictures, for she had created the man I am in a relationship with today.

Devante and I took our first trip together not long after he moved in. We decided to go to New York because that had always been on our bucket lists. We went during December, so that we could see Rockefeller Plaza and the great big Christmas tree. I was also a huge fan of Sex and the City, which takes place in New York, so this was a dream for me. You see, when I first moved to the metro, years ago, I had no money to do much of anything with, and I never got to go out, unless I went on dates. So, I would watch the DVD collection of Sex and the City, seasons 1-6, that Kristen had loaned me. Watching SATC made me feel like I was out, one of the girls, and it got me through many quiet evenings when Bri would be tucked in bed, and I had the rest of the night to myself.

I saw a bit of myself in each one of the girls of SATC. Sometimes I was hopeful Charlotte, believing in love and marriage because my own parents were still together. Sometimes I was Samantha, throwing caution to the wind and having fun with guys for only one thing, because they had proven to me that that was all they were good for. Sometimes I was Miranda, a cynic, hating everything about intimacy and living in the real moments. You could **count** on the real moments; they didn't let you down. Then again, sometimes I was Carrie, the writer who was a bit self-centered, the one who said, and I quote: **"I'm looking for love, real love. Ridiculous, inconvenient, consuming, can't live without each other love."** I also loved to write and had hoped one day I would be free to do so whenever I wanted. And during those long, summer nights at home, I hoped maybe one day I would find my real love.

It would seem I found that real love, and he was taking me to New York. By the time we went, I had seen all six seasons of SATC at least 25 times. When we ordered a fancy car to take us from the airport to our Airbnb, and saw Central Park, I felt a tear roll down my cheek. It sounds kind of silly, I know, but I thought about how far I had come from those nights of watching that show. I was at home because I had no money to go out with. I had a little tv with rabbit ears, empty cupboards that food was supposed to go in, my car was always on empty, and if Brianna got any treats, it was when she came to Caribou and I gave her my shift drink, turning it into an Oreo Snowdrift instead of a coffee for myself. Now here I was, in a fancy black stretch, and I was traveling past the places I had only ever seen on TV in my show. I had a good, kind, and wonderful man at my side, I had put on a little weight because, clearly, our cupboards were now full of food. The car always was full of gas, and Bri was treated to Stone Cold Creamery when she wanted ice creams.

It's hard to fully describe a moment like that, and here I am, the writer, unable to tell you how much that moment in time impacted me. It was bittersweet really. Waves of emotion washed over me, and when I looked at Devante, his eyes mirrored my own wonderment at the big city. He knew what I was thinking, I know he did. Years before, I had told him about my SATC nights, and now, as we drove by Central Park, I looked out my window and pressed my lips together to keep my watery eyes from betraying me even more.

When we were finally at our destination, we dropped off our bags and took a walk in the city. I felt like I was home, this was where I belonged. We did do all the touristy things, like 66 Perry Street, where Carrie Bradshaw's walk-up was. We saw Freedom Tower, and the bull on Wall Street; we went to the Empire State Building, we saw the Rockefeller Plaza Christmas tree. We met up with a friend of mine and he took us to Queens, where we had some interesting and delicious South American food. We did so many fun things, and when we had to return to Minnesota, we vowed to go back as soon as time and work allowed.

We did end up going up going back to New York a year and a half later. We went in the summer this time, and we brought Brianna. I was elated to know that we would be in New York at the same time as the Mermaid Parade on Coney Island. I had developed a love for mermaids over the years. It started with me liking the idea of Sirens mostly. They were like the evil twin sisters of mermaids. They would lure men to their drowning deaths, all with their beauty and their songs. I liked that thought. I wouldn't say I was a man-hater, but I didn't think there were many good ones, that was for sure. I liked that men were so stupidly ruled by their desires, that they would willingly jump ship to their deaths at the hint of a sexual encounter. The Siren, in my mind, represented the taking back of power by women; the ability of women to give men what they truly deserved. Over time, and having met Devante, I started to adore mermaids as well. They were fun, and beautiful, and good. They were the perfect yin to the Siren's yang. So, as you can probably tell, I was overjoyed at attending this function. It was a spectacular time, and I have many photos from that day.

Bri also fell in love with New York and didn't want to return home. She was free in New York, free to be whomever she wanted. She was surrounded by dreams and lights and opportunity. New York changed things for all of us. It was the catalyst that allowed us to see what could be ahead. We discovered that we were all good at traveling together, and that between the three of us, we had some fairly large dreams.

"It doesn't cost anything to dream, so dream big."

~ Magaly Vargas

"One belongs to New York instantly, one belongs to it as much in five minutes as in five years."

~Tom Wolfe

One Dream at a Time

On my birthday, in August of 2018, Devante bought me a MacBook Pro. I was elated. I finally had my own laptop, and I could write to my heart's content. We had also decided that I would be able to give my notice at work and stay home so I could write. I was very thankful for this opportunity, and although at first, I worried about what society would think about me not working, I finally squared my chin, and decided that it didn't matter. People work out what their relationship looks like between themselves, and them alone. I didn't need to justify our decision to anyone. If this decision made me happy, and if Devante was happy, that is what mattered.

At first, it was difficult to make the initial decision. I knew I would be dependent on him, and I had to trust that he would not use that to his advantage or treat me any differently. The slightest thing said, would be taken at face value, so he also needed to be on board with things that may come up. I also had to trust that we would be together for a long time, longer than my usual four year maximum. I had to trust that we were truly committed, and for a girl who consistently lost everything, that was the hardest part.

Our decision was surprising to me at first. We consider ourselves very progressive individuals, and to have these more traditional roles in our home was interesting. We had many discussions about it, and determined that for us, being progressive doesn't always mean to shun traditional values or ideas. Some of the best situations do involve traditional roles. Had I had the career, and Devante had been the writer, it is very probable that I would be working, and he would be the one who would write freely.

Once we got the kinks worked out, I decided to start my own website, where I could feature my blogs and poems and anything else I was doing creatively. I spent hours getting it "just right," and I dreamed of maybe even making some money off my talents. I blogged away at first, and my friends were kind enough to read, comment and share my posts. Social media is a beast though, and the people I thought would support me, didn't. I knew that people were busy, and leading their own lives, so I tried not to take any of it personally. I was also frustrated because I saw them sharing other things, but when it came to my writing, only my closest friends and my daughter would share. It was hard not to feel resentful, especially when they asked people to support ***their*** endeavors, and I usually did. In addition, it was a bit of a blow to my pride and a huge dose of reality when I saw how little traffic I was generating with my writing.

Over time, I accepted that not everyone was into reading blogs, and it would have to just be for my own enjoyment. These days, people are interested in sound bites, quick little videos, and infographics. Any monetary or public recognition would be the cherry on top of my already fortunate life.

Then came writer's block. It's a real thing. I had nothing I wanted to say or write about, I was distracted with the past. I rarely went home to visit because doing so always made me feel uncomfortable. I hated the area up north, and I still felt shame where my parents were concerned. I still had feelings of low self-esteem and going up north seemed to bring those feelings to the forefront. I would go and visit with Chloe and the kids, but I didn't stay with my parents much. I felt awkward and things felt so forced on my end. My parents were kind and welcoming, and they liked Devante a lot. I just felt like the black sheep, and so most of the time, if I wanted to visit with Mom and Dad, I would bring plenty of wine to deal with the atmosphere. My brother lived across the road from my parents, and he would usually be there. Since there was no love lost between us, it didn't make for pleasant evenings with all of us in my opinion.

I spent a lot of time feeling upset about my past, and the things I went through. Denial had taken its course earlier in life while I partied away and escaped the reality of things. Now, anger and depression had settled in during the last few years. Like a pesky pimple, it rose to a head. I became irritable and snappy, and started finding fault with just about everything. At first, I chalked it up to perimenopause. I was sure I was just starting the change of life, and that annoyed the hell out of me. I was too young! But no, I was not too young, however, and I didn't think this was all due to hormones. I was acutely aware of my anger toward men, anger toward my parents for not protecting me, anger at my brother for judging me, and anger at myself for being ruled by my emotions.

Oddly, it was during this time in my life, that something miraculous happened, involving the baby I had placed in adoption so many years ago. His name was Joey, I knew that much, but there was so much more to come. I had told Anthony and Chloe about him many years ago, when I knew they could handle the information. I had told Bri just a few years ago, and she was excited at the thought of having another older brother. She was so excited, that as she got older and acquired her own Instagram, she took to creeping on **his** Instagram. Touch screens are sometimes sensitive, and she accidentally "liked" one of his photos. She came to me in a full-on panic.

"Mom! I accidentally liked one of Joey's photos! Should I unlike it?" If you post a photo on Instagram, and someone liked it, you got a notification of who that someone was. Bri knew this, and she was now looking at me with wide eyes and a grimace on her face. Because I wasn't sure how much Joey knew about his adoption, if anything at all, I closed my eyes in frustration and took a deep breath before I answered.

"No," I said quietly. "Just leave it. It might draw more attention to unlike it since it's been a few hours."

It became apparent that Joey had seen Brianna's blunder, because one by one, he started following each of the kids on Instagram and they excitedly followed him back. Anthony, Chloe, and Bri were so elated, and as I saw their joy and Joey's obvious willingness for a connection, I felt an aching in my heart. This was bittersweet. To be put back together, one's falling apart is often times on full display. My past failure at being able to raise my own child was again brought to the forefront of my mind, and I was humbled by my flaws. Below is how reconnection came to be:

(Sarita Vargas, I Once Held You in My Arms, November 18, 2021, www.saritasiren.com/myadoptionjourney)

"July of 2019, I got a call from my dad. Joey's mom had contacted them, as they didn't know how to reach me, and told him that Joey had expressed an interest in getting to know his birth family. She was wondering if I was ok with this. Was I ok with this???? I had only waited for literally decades for this moment! I was given her phone number, and I was invited to call her to discuss.

In the meantime, everything with the kids just fell into place. They started talking on social media, friending each other and Joey even started a group chat with Anthony, Chloe, and Bri. I know he was testing the waters and going at his own pace, and I had to respect that. He did not reach out to me, not immediately. My kids shared a bit with me, just in general, about their conversations with him, but they were thick as thieves, keeping him to themselves, hungrily making up for lost time. I was just happy that it was all happening, and that I could see all four of them finally being able to connect.

It wasn't long after that that Joey and I communicated. Conversations were too long for texting, and, not yet ready for a phone call, we emailed instead. We learned a lot from each other, about each other. I think I was on cloud nine for days. I learned that Joey was a good-hearted person, and he assured me that he held no resentment or anger toward me. I was relieved to hear that, because I felt so undeserving and so sorry for the choice I had to make. He understood and let me know he had a good up-bringing, and it was ok. I cried so much during that time because I wouldn't have blamed him if he had hated me.

It was that summer that I was finally able to meet Joey in person. Again. It is not lost on me that so many adoption stories end sadly, tragically even, and that I am a very blessed woman. Not only did I find my own birth mother and establish a rewarding relationship with her, but I have also been given the chance to be reunited with the son I placed for adoption so long ago. I feel unworthy and humbled by this whole experience.

The meeting would be up north, at my parent's home. This way he could reunite with his biological Nana and Grandfather, and his uncle Aaron and his cousins. I prayed it wouldn't be too overwhelming for him, and that it would be alright. My heart was pounding so loudly, I swear you could hear it across the state! We made the drive from Minneapolis to Britt, Minnesota, and as we pulled into the driveway, there he was. He was tall, dark, and handsome. He was smiling, and his hair- oh he has amazing hair!! Hahaha! I couldn't get out of the car fast enough.

Suddenly I was aware of myself and all my flaws. Would he be disappointed? Would he think I'm ugly? Would he think I am good enough? Those fears disappeared the instant he wrapped me in his arms in a big hug. It was then that I think a million different moments flashed through my mind: my dad's face as he had that talk with me 22 years ago. My sad, forlorn little apartment, the eviction-notice on my door, the faces of Anthony and Chloe and Brianna all morphed together and turning into Joey. The letters in the mail from his mother. The photos in my hand of him as a child. The feelings of being alone at the hospital. The look on his mother's face as she thanked me through tears at my hospital bedside. The joy of discovering his talents in the music world. The elation at knowing he wanted to be a part of our lives. The fear of rejection. And finally, the realization of love that never went away but was still new somehow. All of that in that one hug, and the laughter and smiles afterward. I couldn't get enough of him. I studied every body movement, every tilt of his head, every word, every smile, every mannerism. Some looked very familiar, some were only faintly familiar, and some were not familiar at all.

We visited and laughed into the evening with my parents. What I wouldn't have given to have my own birth mother there to meet her grandson as well. But that's a selfish thought given how blessed I already was, isn't it. We had so many questions, and we answered so many questions. We met his friend Lyndzie and even his brother Zach. What an amazing day and evening this was! We celebrated with food and wine and coffee and music and everyone talking all at once. It was a proper family get together, and we meshed well from the beginning. Joey did tell me that he noticed when Brianna liked one of his pics on Instagram, and he was intrigued. I think that was maybe the instance for him that gave an already formulated thought momentum.

Over the months and years, we have had many visits. Each visit has taught me more about Joey, and more about myself as well. I've even seen Anthony, Chloe, and Bri in different lights. Joey is the one that binds them together, it would seem. He was the missing piece of our puzzle. I look at photos of all four of the kids- each one looks like the next, yet they all have their own distinct personalities with similarities among them. Joey is gentle like Anthony, free spirited like Chloe, sarcastic and creative like Bri, and yet he brings his own things to the table. He is a talented musician and quick and confident... I love watching the kids all together because somehow, they just make sense that way. You know?"

Finally meeting Joey and having that part of my life start to mend, opened my eyes to how much I was loved. I started to see that little by little, moment by moment, God was working behind the scenes and putting my life back together from all the fragmented pieces that abuse, trauma, self-hatred and loss had strewn all over. He had started with the very first trauma in my own life, being placed in adoption decades ago in 1973, and He kept going with the private and aching trauma of placing my own baby in adoption. Come fall, He would take a key token of my brokenness, and gently make it the one that the rest of life would surround.

It was that year, in November, that Devante and I went on a trip to Spain. We chose Spain because it was the motherland. I was Spanish, and even Devante was, so this trip was going to be meaningful for us both to see where our ancestors came from. We chose to go to Barcelona, because not only was it a beautiful city, but Devante had visited it long ago as a child. Barcelona did not disappoint; everywhere we went, there was beauty all around.

We had so many great experiences there and saw so many amazing places. One place we went to had been high on my bucket list. It was Park Güell, which consisted of gardens and sculptures and was designed by Antoni Gaudí. It's whimsical and arty, so I was in heaven when we bought our tickets. We arrived early in the morning, which was the perfect time to go. It was peaceful, and the air was crisp and clean. The sun was already out, trying to warm up the earth as we made our way through the mazes and nooks and crannies that were Park Güell.

We went up some outdoor stairs that led to a view of all of Barcelona, with the Mediterranean Sea in the distance. Nearby, there was a small hill that had three crosses on it, **Cerro de las Tres Cruces**. These crosses represented Calgary and the three crosses, one of which belonged to Jesus. Devante shared my love for Jesus, which I'm thankful for. It amazed me that throughout all my abuse, when things were happening to me that no-one deserves to have happen, I never was angry at God. I somehow knew that He had no fault in any of this, and if anything saved me from myself, it was God, beyond any doubt.

It was there that Devante got down on one knee and asked me to marry him. I will never forget the look of hope on his face that day, and the immense love he had in his eyes when he looked at me. I knew in that moment, he saw me. He saw the real me- flaws and strengths both, and he accepted everything that came with me. I did not even have to think about it, I said yes.

We Are All in This Together

On the way back from Spain, on the flight home, I felt myself become sicker and sicker. The plane was huge, and I was fighting my gag reflexes when I thought about all the germs. I was warm- hot even. I was coming down with something, and it wasn't good. My body temperature was rising, and my throat was sore. By the time we re-entered the States and got a cab for home, I was miserable.

I spent two weeks in bed. I had never had a flu like the one I had upon our return. My throat hurt, but I had no white spots on it to indicate strep. All I could do was sleep, which was not normal for me, even when I had a bad cold or flu. I had no energy; I could barely eat soup. I was coughing continuously, but there wasn't really any phlegm. I felt like death.

Then, when I finally started to come around, Devante went down. I was going to have to bring our dog Zeus out for potty, which Devante usually did. Zeus was massive, and quite the guard dog. You had to be strong and firm with him because he could seriously kill someone. He weighed in at a whopping 165 pounds of solid muscle, and although he was neutered, he was still ready to fight if need be. I could handle Zeus when I was at 100%, but after the illness I went through, I was probably at 45%. I prayed that Zeus would not be an asshole, because I was still so weak. I brought him out the back way. There was no elevator there, and that meant fewer neighbors. It was the safest option though, at this point. We lived on the third floor, and when I brought him back in, I had to rest on the landing of each set of stairs, due to my body still feeling very weak.

Devante's sickness was very much the same as mine: exhaustion, excessive non-productive coughing, shortness of breath, and the desire to sleep. It took over a month for us both to start feeling like our old selves. That was in November. By January, we were starting to hear about this new flu that was spreading rapidly. Devante and I looked at each other as we watched the news, and although the first known case of Covid-19 here in the States was technically January 30, we couldn't help but wonder how many cases were here that they didn't know about prior to. Were we spreaders? Had we in fact, caught this new flu and didn't know it? Neither of us were big on going to the doctor, so we hadn't gone in. We had just ridden it out at home. Brianna didn't get sick at all, but she never got sick. We knew that Europe had had many cases, and we were just there.

As Covid-19 cases climbed in number, and the world became more stressed out, we also started wondering what the future had in store. By March, we were in a state of emergency and things were shutting down right and left. School was a mess, jumbling its way to online access. Devante had to work from home now, as offices were staying closed so as not spread the disease. I had been working part-time at Lifetime

Fitness, in the spa, and that, too, had to close. Pretty soon, the only places that were open were grocery stores, liquor stores, and gas stations.

We were being given a bunch of different advice and information as Covid spread more and more, and they were learning new things on a weekly, if not daily basis. People were dying, dying from this disease. It became a very scary world, and people started to panic. Going to the grocery store involved wearing masks, it was mandatory now. Many people started washing their groceries when they brought them home, disinfecting them, and taking their clothes off at the door, so they could throw them into the washing machine immediately.

Amid the changes to our world, and the quietness of the once loud streets and shopping centers, people started to get restless. It's inevitable, when the freedoms everyone was used to had to be put aside for the "greater good," there was bound to be backlash. This was also the era of the Trump presidency, and we experienced division amongst the people of our country to a degree that I had never seen before. People were fighting about race and borders. Anger was at an all-time high. Now we had people getting angry because they couldn't go anywhere without having to wear a mask. We had people going to extremes to avoid others, Instacart boomed with business because no one wanted to go out. No one without a car could go out because Ubers and Lyfts and busses weren't running.

It was during this time, this horrible time, Devante's mother passed. It happened faster than we anticipated, and we couldn't even be by her side. Everyone was sheltered in place, and borders to other countries were closed. Instead, like many others that year who lost family members, we had to be by her side via Facebook Messenger's video calling. Devante sat on the couch, his back curved from the weight of the world, talking to his mother, and comforting her. I sat with him, and when we had a moment to take a break, I did the only thing I could do. I made some homemade chicken soup, hoping he would at least eat and get his strength up, so broken was his spirit. When she left us, I had no idea that for the first time ever, I would learn what it meant to be loyal, unselfish, and patient when it came to a man in my life.

Like I said earlier, Devante was working from home, and his little office space was in our room. I decided we needed to move him out to the living room, I could not stand to see him in our bedroom all day and all night after what he went through. I did my best to comfort him, but so detached from emotion was I from my own junk, that it was a new and foreign concept to me to witness someone go through the emotions that happen when it comes to losing their one and only parent. I Googled for help, I wanted to do and say the things that were right, things that would help him and not do further damage.

Along with Devante coping with the loss of his mother, we were also coping with the reality of life during the pandemic. I had a circle of friends I could no longer spend time with for a break from the sad energy in our home. We had managed to move in the middle of all of this, because our lease was coming up at our apartment. We needed to be gone from that little place, it held the memory of Magaly's passing, and we couldn't get out from under that.

We moved into a big home in Plymouth, on a quiet street. It was good timing because I think we all needed a little space from each other. Bri was back in school, attending online like everyone else. They were now vaccinating people against Covid, and things were opening back up at a snail's pace. We learned to get along, all of us, because we had no choice. I was seeing Devante every day now, and vice-versa. He now had an office, and that helped. It was a weird time, because although we were getting along, there was underlying stress at the helm.

The world was fighting. In the States, division was escalating. People had lost their homes because they couldn't go to work. Some people had avoided eviction due to a bill that was put in place, preventing people from being kicked out of their apartments for being unable to meet rent. There was still stress though, because without work, people couldn't buy groceries. People were arguing about masks. It was still mandatory to wear them if you wanted to visit businesses that were starting to open their doors, and there were people who would refuse to wear the mask, saying that they felt it violated their personal rights. Then there were people who felt like it was violating their personal rights to be exposed to the people who refused to wear a mask.

Friendships broke apart, families started arguing and not getting together anymore, and it made many people feel they had to choose between "science or family." In our own family- mine, it caused many heated conversations, and I saw some shocking behavior from myself and my family members as well. Tensions ran high, and my friend group went through a crack in the circle. It was tough times, because not only were people losing friends and family to divided opinions, but they were literally losing friends and family to Covid. I had a friend who was a nurse, crying and telling me of the horrors she witnessed with a hospital full of patients dying from Covid, and I had other friends telling me that our bodies would fight it naturally and we needed to let it run its course. I had other friends telling me science, science, science; and still other friends who basically just went into hiding to avoid the world altogether. It was a mess. Covid was vicious, and it got to a point where we all just wanted it to stop.

Those times added up to about a year and a half of complete garbage. But hey, at least we were all in it together, right?

36

Aria

As the waters of the pandemic started to calm, and the world started to navigate the aftermath, Devante and I had come to an impasse. I truly believe the pandemic had taken a toll on us both, on top of the grief he was dealing with from losing his mother. I watched as he struggled, and when it was evident that his struggle was affecting him, and as a result, us, I suggested therapy. The great Me, who could not make it through five sessions without quitting, suggested therapy so he could "fix himself." How arrogant it was on my part, to assume this was all his doing, yet that was where I was. Oh, we weren't arguing much, but my dissatisfaction with myself and projecting that his way, and his grief and personal struggles of the last years and me not being as supportive as I could be, brought us to this place of a great shadow across our relationship.

Devante, being the responsible man he is, did go ahead and seek therapy. I was feeling a bit sheepish, truthfully, as I watched him faithfully attend his appointments. I started to see him change, and a new kind of peace was coming over him. Not to be outdone, I magnanimously offered to go to therapy as well. There was no way I was going to let him become a better person without me also becoming a better person. Once the feeling of generosity wore off, I sighed when I realized I would have to begin the hunt for a therapist, again.

I sat back in my chair and looked at my life in its entirety. Here I was, no longer the little brown girl from Northern Minnesota; I was a woman, just about to turn 49. I was a Grammy, a mother, a friend, a lover, a grown-up. My children were grown, and soon I would enter the time of life where I could rest and enjoy the years prior. Brianna was going into her senior year at school, and if I didn't get my mind right, she would graduate and move on, and I would be left with myself and my dark past.

Someone posted the following on social media: "You are responsible for how long you let what hurt you, haunt you."

I had all kinds of feelings about this. It is true, to a degree. Once we are aware that there is a problem that we are at the core of, in many cases, we are now responsible for finding a solution. Yet, when emotional growth is stunted because of said problems, it can be impossible to be able to utilize whatever gumption, tools, or otherwise in our possession to seek help in overcoming these problems. I was up against myself for many, many years, decades even. In many ways, Devante's love for me was one of the things that helped me. I wish I could say I did this all on my own, but I did not. Whether I acknowledged it or not, I was in a relationship that gave me what it was that I needed to be able to start loving myself. When you love yourself, you start taking care of yourself. Up until meeting Devante, I truly did not see that I was a person deserving of love. Oh, I wanted the kind of love that I hoped was out there, but I didn't know how to recognize it, even if it was living right under the same roof.

Over time, I did mature in many ways, and even without Devante, I believe that I would have reached the point where I was able to start healing all on my own. I might be 90 years old by that time, but it probably would have happened. His love just helped propel the process. My growth was slow going, but it was happening. By the time I met Devante, I knew that what I was doing wasn't working. If I wanted something different, I had to do things differently. Watching him now as he grew and benefited from his therapy gave me courage to fill out the form online that would change things for me, forever.

The therapists I could choose from had bios that I read through. I knew I wanted a female, for obvious reasons. If I was able to talk about the things I had gone through, and even the things I couldn't bring myself to remember, it would need to be with a woman. I sent my request through and waited a reply. I heard back almost immediately, and I was connected to the therapist I had inquired about. She spoke with me briefly on the phone, and after hearing a very condensed version of what I was looking for, she stated that she felt I probably suffered from PTSD. I wasn't opposed to this possibility. I knew I was going through it, and my issues with sex, men, power, and control were only lying dormant while I was being loved by Devante.

The therapist felt I would be a better match with Andie, a woman who was an expert with PTSD and used a method of therapy called EMDR. EMDR is basically short for Eye Movement Desensitization and Reprocessing. It's a type of therapy that is relatively new, but it has had a great amount of success. Essentially, while going over events that have caused trauma, the patient will sometimes use a tapping method while their eyes are closed. It's rhythmic and gentle, and somehow helps the brain process the trauma in a safe environment, with the guide of a professionally trained expert. Other times, the patient will follow a bilateral pattern with their eyes as they process trauma, again, guided by a therapist who specializes in EMDR. Either one of these methods helps to put trauma in a "proper" location within the brain, thus preventing it from bouncing around in your thoughts on a daily basis- very much like a pinball machine. Now, instead of chaos, the brain is quieter, the noise of trauma disappears over time.

So, there I was, setting my first appointment for a new kind of therapy. I felt like this was make or break time for me as well. If I didn't go through with it this time around, I probably would never go through with it. I looked at Devante as he sat outside, waiting on the grill to heat up. He looked happy and I felt a surge of comfort and love. I respected him so much, and he was such an example of doing what needed to be done, that I vowed to try in therapy as much as I could, even though that meant I would be extremely uncomfortable. I would do it in honor of him, in honor of us, in honor of my children, but most firstly, and most importantly, in honor of myself.

The day of my session came all too quickly. I nervously gathered my laptop and went downstairs into the spare bedroom. I closed the door and wrapped a blanket around my shoulders. I wanted to be comfy, warm, surrounded. I had a cup of hot tea, and I was ready. Like most therapy first sessions, this one consisted mostly of she and I getting acquainted, and me telling her a little bit about what I hoped to gain from our time together. What did I want? I wanted peace. I wanted to be out from under this "past" being on my shoulders all the time. I wanted a day where I just felt like going shopping, or cooking, or maybe going for a walk, without my past in the back of my mind. I wanted to let it go, once and for all. I wanted my past to be something I chose to think about, and not something that I was thinking about constantly, as habit. I wanted to love myself, I wanted to forgive myself. I didn't want to be triggered by things that were non-threatening. Please help, I said silently in my mind.

Andie was very kind, very gentle, and very insightful. She laid out a plan for us and said that we could deviate from the plan at any time, if it became apparent that I needed to. The plan involved setting a timeline of events in my life, things that had traumatized me, or moments when I lost time. Yes, I lost time. There were huge chunks of time that I blocked out; months, sometimes years, where I didn't know what I was doing or where I was living. We would go through and address the traumatic moments, and we would process the feelings that came with the blocked-out moments. I was scared, but I was hopeful.

EMDR, for me, looked like this: I would sit with my hands crossed over my chest, my fingertips on the opposite shoulders. I would close my eyes and recall memories, and while Andie broke those memories up in bits and pieces, I would tap my shoulders lightly with the opposite fingertips, alternating taps. We would discuss a moment, and I would talk about how I felt. I didn't even have to make sense. I could just say words if I wanted. The great thing about this, was that my eyes would need to be closed. This helped me immensely. I would not have to look at the person I was telling these things to, it was almost like she wasn't there at all.

Over the course of time, Andie got very good at determining when I needed a break, even if, true to my personality, I wanted to soldier on. There were days when I would sit in therapy and just cry while we processed a trauma. I would tap, and the tears would fall from my face. Those days felt very heavy. I wanted to quit many times, and I almost gave up for real. It was then that I would remind myself, I am worth it. Be kind to yourself and do this so you can be free. You can do this.

And so, I would go on, and to Devante's credit, he would never pry, but would always let me know he was there if I ever wanted to discuss. Some days, after a therapy session, I would be so exhausted that I would have to go lay down and take a nap. Some days, I would come out to the living room and just zone out in front of some mindless TV show. Other days, I would come out of therapy, eyes swollen and red, and Devante would just hold me while I cried. He let me just cry into his shoulder and he would tell me that he was so proud of me. I cried more in the last ten months than I had in my whole life.

Andie also suggested that I journal. She said that it was a good way to write down my feelings, to give myself an outlet. That was when the idea for this book was born. I am naturally drawn to writing with the intent that it will be read by others, and I had always wanted to "explain" to the people that grew up with me, the people who knew me or knew of me, as to why I was the way I was. I wanted to tell my story, in a sense, because I hoped it would help others, and help me. I just could not, up until now.

Previously, I had started writing a novel, and had gotten a few chapters in, when I experienced writer's block. I couldn't bring myself to pick it up again, let alone come up with story that made sense. This time, with this book, I sat down, and hours would slip by as I wrote and wrote and wrote. It almost felt like this book was writing itself. I recounted the events as I remembered them, and the ones I couldn't bring to the surface, I just wrote about a general feeling. Even with Andie, I couldn't recall certain times in my life, like- who took my virginity for example. I still cannot recall that, yet somehow, it doesn't matter. I have processed the feelings that I have about that loss and have also changed my view on virginity as well.

At the time I write this, I am still going to therapy, and I probably will be for a while longer. It takes a long time to process 49 years of life. I know there will be times where my past may try and hold me captive or make me feel like I'm "less than," but now I am developing the tools I need to put these memories in the file cabinets where they belong. I will take them out when I need to, but I do not feel like I'll need these fragmented memories much longer. Soon, I hope that they will collect dust because they will be a distant, fleeting memory.

I smile as I look back at the way I so "kindly" offered to go to therapy as well, what a pompous ass I was! Devante and I laugh about it now, but in truth, regardless of our situation, I needed therapy desperately. It has helped me see the world through a different set of eyes, and I feel fortunate to still have many good years in front of me with which to enjoy the freedoms that are being unlocked, one therapy session at a time.

What I am thankful for, are the relationships I am now nurturing and caring for. Devante has been the most supportive human being I've ever encountered, and we just celebrated seven years together, which for me, is a record. Also, my children and I have always been close, but it has been in the last six or seven years that I have become even closer to each one of them. We are a family, and everyone in our family is accepted. I'll never judge their decision making, instead, I try and approach their minds and hearts with love and support. We may not always agree with each other on choices or opinions, but we support each other to the very end.

"You've always been my safe place," my daughter Chloe said to me recently. She had been watching a show on Netflix and begged me to watch it, because the mother reminded her of me, and the dynamics in the family reminded her of her youth. She has since said that even through the instability of my love life and the crazy things I've done, she's always thought I was such a bad-ass. It was nice to hear, because I told her that as I write this book, it seems like my life consisted of one bad mistake after another, and it was nice to know I was thought of or seen differently by my children.

As I go into the next phase of life, with my now husband Devante by my side, I have hope; hope for a life free from the ties that bind us to our painful pasts, hope for the days I feel are right around the corner. The little brown girl who had no boundaries, is now the brown woman who is learning to put boundaries in place, and not feel guilty about doing so. That little brown girl is now a brown woman with a voice. I have decided to show grace for erstwhile friends who have chosen to distance themselves from me, whether out of judgement, or for their own mental health reasons. I have forgiven the family members who have inadvertently hurt me and have peace with the decision to exclude certain ones from my life. I have forgiven myself for not being able to love and receive love for much of my existence. I have taken a deep breath; I have decided to live a new life. My Aria is like the one I heard long ago when I was just a 17-year-old girl, soaring high in triumph and beauty for all the world to hear.

The End...
is only the beginning.

If you have been abused, or suspect that you have been abused, or if you know someone who needs help, do not hesitate to reach out!

National Sexual Assault Hotline: 1-800-656-4673 or visit rainn.org

Victim Connect Center: call or text 1-855-484-2846 or visit victimconnect.org

Crisis Text Line: Text HOME to 741741 or visit crisistextline.org

References:

The Metropolitan Opera, accessed 02/2023 [https://www.metopera.org/discover/education/educator-guides/agrippina/10-essential-musical-terms/#:~:text=Aria,many%20arias%20include%20musical%20repetition]

April Goff, 2021, "Hypersexuality [sic] and Sex Repulsion", fortraumasurvivors.com, accessed February 2023 [https://www.fortraumasurvivors.com/post/hypersexuality-and-sex-repulsion]

Sara McLean, June 2016, "The Effect of Trauma on the Brain Development of Children", Australian Government/Australian Institute of Family Studies, accessed February 2023 [https://aifs.gov.au/resources/practice-guides/effect-trauma-brain-development-children#:~:text=Certain%20areas%20of%20the%20frontal,targeted%20interventions%20well%20into%20adolescence]

Kelsie Smith Hayduk, 7 December 2022, "Researchers reveal how trauma changes the brain." University of Rochester Medical Center. ScienceDaily. ScienceDaily, accessed February 2023 [www.sciencedaily.com/releases/2022/12/221207142255.htm]

Shonagh Walker and Sara Mulcahy, May 2022, "Coping With Loss: the 7 Stages of Grief", HCF, accessed February 2023 [https://www.hcf.com.au/health-agenda/body-mind/mental-health/moving-through-grief]

Cleveland Clinic medical professional, 29 March 2022, "What is EMDR", Cleveland Clinic, accessed December 2022 [https://my.clevelandclinic.org/health/treatments/22641-emdr-therapy]

Collaborative Therapeutic Services, "What is EMDR", Collaborative Therapeutic Services, accessed December 2022 [https://www.therapycts.com/emdr]

Sarita Vargas, 18 November 2021, "I Once Held You in My Arms…My Adoption Story Pt. 2", Sarita Siren Sounding Off On Life, accessed January 2023 [https://www.saritasiren.com/post/i-once-held-you-in-my-arms-my-adoption-story-pt-2]

www.ingramcontent.com/pod-product-compliance
Lightning Source LLC
Chambersburg PA
CBHW070241010526
44107CB00041B/1485/J